STARGAZING

WITH

MARK THOMPSON

PHILIP'S

STARGAZING
WITH
MARK THOMPSON

THE ESSENTIAL GUIDE TO ASTRONOMY

Mark Thompson is one of the presenters on the RTS nominated show BBC *Stargazing LIVE* (together with Professor Brian Cox and Dara Ó Briain). He is also a specialist presenter on ITV's *This Morning* and a regular on Radio 5 Live. Mark has also been a contributor on *The Sky at Night*, *The Alan Titchmarsh Show* and *The Culture Show*, and now enjoys bringing the beauty of the night sky down to Earth through many different outlets. Embracing social networking media, Mark 'tweets' regularly with more than 67,000 followers (@PeoplesAstro).

Published in Great Britain in 2014 by Philip's,
a division of Octopus Publishing Group Limited
(www.octopusbooks.co.uk)
Endeavour House, 189 Shaftesbury Avenue,
London WC2H 8JY
An Hachette UK Company (www.hachette.co.uk)

ISBN 978–1–84907–313–4

A CIP catalogue record for this book is available from the British Library.

Printed in China

Details of other Philip's titles can be found on our website at: www.philipsastronomy.com

ACKNOWLEDGEMENTS
Alamy /Philip Bird 29, /blickwinkel 142, 152b, /Linda Matlow 11, /Nature Picture Library 143, /Dale O'Dell 159, /Pere Sanz 138, /Stocktrek Images, Inc. 8, 31, 43, 45, 54, 57, 61, 63, 140b, 161t, /Richard Wainscoat 129, /Reinhold Wittich 40, 49; **Mike Brown** 145; **Celestron** (www.celestron.com) 82b, 110; **DMR/COBE/NASA/Two-year Sky Map** 170; **ESA/AOES Medialab** 135; **ESA/ C. Carreau** 134; **Galaxy Picture Library** /Paul Andrew 74, /Matthew Boulton 136, /Jamie Cooper 146, /Eddie Guscott 166, /Yoji Hirose 69b, 139t, 139b, /Geir T. Øye 73, /Ian Palmer 97, /Damian Peach 66b, 126, 152t, /Philip Perkins 168, /Emma Porter 3 (background), 137, /Robin Scagell 66t, 67t, 70, 75, 76, 77t, 84t, 84b, 90, 96, 106, 109b, 115, 116, 118, 149, 165, /Peter Shah 67b, 68b, 163, 164, 167, /Dave Tyler 6b, 140t, /Erwin van der Velden 125t; **The Hubble Heritage Team (AURA/STScI/NASA)** 68t, 130; **S. Kafka and K. Honeycutt, Indiana University/WIYN/NOAO/NSF** 160t; **Losmandy Astronomical Products** (www.losmandy. com) 99; **NASA** 78; **NASA and The Hubble Heritage Team (STScI/AURA)** 65b, 127b, 153; **NASA, ESA, S. Beckwith (STScI), and The Hubble Heritage Team (STScI/AURA)** 69t; **NASA, ESA, CFHT, CXO, M. J. Jee (University of California, Davis) and A. Mahdavi (San Francisco State University)** 5, 6t, 10t, 34t, 76t, 94, 108t, 124, 144t, 172, 174; **NASA/ESA/I. de Pater and M. Wong (University of California, Berkeley)** 127t; **NASA, ESA, STScI, J. Hester and P. Scowen (Arizona State University)** 16; **NASA/JPL** 150, 155cr, 157, 158; **NASA/JPL-Caltech/Calvin J. Hamilton** 151; **NASA/JPL-Caltech/SSC** 169; **NASA/JPL/DLR** 155bl, 155br; **NASA/JPL/Lunar and Planetary Laboratory** 155cl; **NASA/JPL/Space Science Institute** 156; **NASA/JPL/University of Arizona** 154; **NASA/USGS** 128; **NSSDC Photo Gallery** 125b; **Optical Vision Ltd** (www.opticalvision.co.uk) 79, 86, 88; **Orion Optics** (www.orionoptics.co.uk) 80b; **Orion Telescopes & Binoculars** (www.telescope.com) 77b; **Shutterstock/gary718** 15; **Society for Popular Astronomy** (www.popastro.com) 133; **Courtesy SOHO/EIT Consortium** 148; **Paul Stephens** 144b; **Swinburne Astronomy Productions/ESO** 81; **Telescope House** (www.telescopehouse.com) 85; **Mark Thompson** 7, 10b, 13t, 19t, 25, 32, 33, 65t, 83, 87, 89, 91, 92, 95t, 95b, 101, 104, 107, 108b, 109t, 112, 113t, 113b, 114, 117t, 117b, 119t, 119b, 120t, 120b, 121t, 121b, 122; **Dave Tyler** 155t.
Photograph of Mark Thompson (© Philip's) taken by Darren Bell (www.darren-bell.co.uk): 3.
Illustrations (© Philip's): 9b, 12, 14, 17, 18, 19b, 20, 24, 26, 34b, 35, 76c, 80t, 82t, 147, 160–161.
Illustrations by Jonathan Bell (© Philip's): 13b, 21, 102, 103, 111.
Star charts by Wil Tirion (© Philip's): 22–23, 30, 37, 39, 41, 42, 44, 47, 48, 50, 51, 53, 55, 56, 58, 60, 62, 64.

CONTENTS

INTRODUCTION

I WAS ABOUT TEN years old the first time I looked through a telescope. What I saw that night was a vision that had somehow transported me through space to an alien world, a *real* alien world. Set against the velvety blackness of space, almost leaping out at me in glorious 3D, was the planet Saturn. I had seen pictures in books and on television, but to see it for real, well, I can only tell you that it set a fire burning deep inside me and that fire is still burning strong and pure, because I still look at the night sky with a childlike wonder. The crazy thing is that I have seen Saturn countless times since, but not once has it seemed as incredible as it did that night. The reality is it probably has looked as good if not better, and I certainly have better equipment now than I did then, but it was the excitement and joy of seeing it for the first time which gave it an extra sparkle.

Since then I have been lucky enough to introduce other people to Saturn and the other planets, and always get a real joy from seeing their reaction. For a few, they will have had their curiosity satisfied and may never look through a telescope again, but for most it sets them off on a journey to learn more about the Universe and to try to find their own way

▲ *Saturn – the sixth planet from the Sun and the object that has inspired my journey to explore the night sky.*

▶ *Through this book, I will help you get started on your exploration of the Universe and all its wonders.*

around the sky. It is a journey that can be quite daunting at the outset and while the thought of navigating around the sky or choosing your first telescope might fill you with dread now, I will make sure that before very long you are hopping around the sky like a pro. Over the years, I have helped hundreds of people get started in astronomy and have seen them progress, but unfortunately I cannot be there to help you in person. Do not panic, though – this book includes everything you need to know. Along the way I will give you loads of little hints and tips that I have picked up over the years, so I can still be your companion and guide you through your early stargazing experiences.

As you will see in Chapter 3, one of the most common questions I get asked by those new to the subject is: 'What telescope should I buy?' My answer to them is always the same: do not rush out and spend your hard-earned cash until you know which type of telescope best suits your interests. A friend of mine decided – against my advice, I hasten to add – to spend thousands of pounds on a telescope before they actually knew how to use one. Sure enough, they got frustrated with it and ended up selling it and losing a few hundred pounds in the process! It is a big decision and one that deserves thought and research, so make sure you read the chapter carefully before heading out to buy your first telescope.

As you work your way through this book, you will find it structured to take you through learning the essential skills that you will need as an astronomer. The first chapter, for example, starts with the basics and teaches you how the sky moves and how you can hop among the stars, slowly homing in on your target. The focus for the rest of the chapter is on a number of other background subjects such as keeping warm, the weather, even a little bit about time, and while I know you will want to get started, time spent here will give you a great foundation to build from. Do not forget, too, that many of the concepts and discoveries that underpin modern astronomy were made before telescopes were invented: the size of the Earth, the distance to the Moon, the passage of time, and even a rough idea of the layout of the Universe!

The rest of the book looks at extending your new-found skills to more advanced techniques, but while we go through the chapters there are some other things you can do to get yourself started. A great way to learn and get further advice and information is to

join your local astronomical society. There are hundreds of groups of like-minded people up and down the country, and for the cost of the annual membership you will not only have access to friendly advice but you will also more than likely forge some new lifelong friendships with others with whom you can enjoy the glory of the Universe. It is worth subscribing to astronomy magazines too, because these monthly publications are a great way of keeping up to date with news and events in the world of astronomy. Along with the news and events sections you will find information about things you can see in the night sky for the coming months, second-hand equipment sales, equipment reviews and all sorts of other great information. Social media sites are also a great source of advice and information. I love using Twitter to share information around – you can find me as @PeoplesAstro and if you get stuck you can always ping me a message and I will do my best to respond.

Whether looking at the sky with just your eyes or later through a telescope, you, like me, may find one of the most inspiring things is understanding the nature of the objects you are looking at. In the closing chapters of this book I concentrate on explaining a little about the science behind the objects you can see and take a look at some observational projects you can get involved in. The projects can be fun and for some people the focus of these activities adds a whole new dimension to the experience. Many of the projects even help out professional astronomers in their quest to understand and decode the Universe. Projects can include monitoring brightness changes in variable stars, searching for comets, long-term observations of planetary atmospheres and even hunting down exploding stars.

It can be really daunting to start a new hobby, particularly a scientific one, but believe me it is really not that hard. Certainly, it can be more challenging if you delve into the heavy science, but the great thing about amateur astronomy is that you can take it to whatever level you wish. You might read this book, glance at the night sky occasionally and become a little more informed than you were before, or you might become one of the dedicated bunch who help out professional astronomers. Whatever level is right for you, I am sure you will enjoy it. 'Amateur astronomy' has been a passion of mine for 30 years and that phrase encapsulates everything about why I do it. The word 'amateur' has its origins in French and means 'for love', and this for me, as I hope it will be for you, builds a beautiful connection between you and the night sky. It is an amazing and wonderful Universe and together we will get you started on one of the most amazing journeys of your life.

◀ *Local astronomical societies are a great place to get help and advice. Attending their group observing sessions and star parties can add a lot of fun to an otherwise solitary activity. This image showing the Milky Way was taken in the United States at the Okie-Tex Star Party near Black Mesa, Oklahoma.*

chapter 1

THE BASICS

A STRONOMY is without doubt one of the oldest of the natural sciences. Its origins go back to the dawning of mankind and the Palaeolithic Era around 2.5 million years ago, when our early ancestors had an awareness of the sky in much the same way that animals do today. Over millions of years, and as mankind became more inquisitive and questioning, our awareness of the Universe slowly grew. That awareness initially took the shape of mythology, of objects in the sky representing gods, and of signs to predict events down on Earth, and it is at this point around 3,500 years ago that we see the birth of what I would consider something resembling the study of astronomy.

The first real observers of the sky are thought to be priests from Mesopotamia, and it was their efforts to correlate objects and events in the sky to happenings on Earth that pushed forward observational astronomy. Naturally, that effort soon evolved into a discipline more akin to astrology, but two subjects soon started to emerge: the prediction of events otherwise known as astrology, and the endeavour to understand the Universe properly, known as astronomy. Much of the real foundation of our knowledge of the Universe was discovered during these early years, long before the telescope was invented by Dutch spectacle-maker Hans Lippershey in 1608.

The way our knowledge of the Universe evolved before telescopes were invented is a great testimony to just how much astronomy can be done with the naked eye. It is as true today as it was all those years ago, as a great many objects are well within the grasp of the beginner who has yet to buy a telescope. Eyes do have limitations, but understanding how they work means it is possible to optimize their use for astronomy. Each one of your eyes is identical in design although there are often variations between them based on

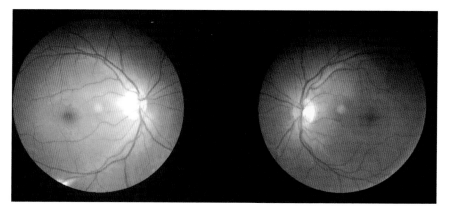

▲ *The retinas of the author's eyes.*

► *A red torch is essential to help keep your eyes adapted to the dark.*

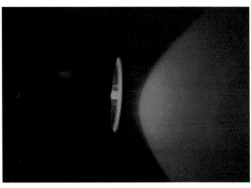

medical conditions or genetic disposition. For example, my right eye is marginally better than my left eye, but both suffer a tiny bit of astigmatism where the front surface of the eye, known as the cornea, is a little misshapen. Behind the cornea of the eye is the iris, which is the coloured bit we are all familiar with, and it has a pretty important function. Look at anyone's eye and you will see a dark hole in the middle of the coloured portion, and it is that dark hole (the 'pupil') where light enters the eye. The function of the iris is to allow less light in if there is bright light or, more crucially for astronomers, to allow more light in if the light levels are low. You can see this for yourself if you sit with a friend in a dark room, then turn the lights on and you will see their pupils contract and get smaller. Moving from a lit room into a darkened environment, as is often the case when starting an observing session, means the eye must adapt to the darkened environment in a process known as *dark adaptation*. The opening up of the iris, where the pupil gets bigger – or dilates, to use the correct term – is the first step and this takes just a few seconds.

Behind the iris and pupil is the lens which takes the incoming light and focuses it through some liquid known as the vitreous gel (whose main function is to keep the eyeball in shape and stop it collapsing) and on to the retina and the light-sensitive detectors. The detectors, which are known as rods and cones, also have to adjust to the darkened environment in the second phase of dark adaptation, but this takes around 40 minutes. For an astronomer's eyes to become fully dark adapted takes a good hour, so patience is

The human eye

Horizontal section through the human eye

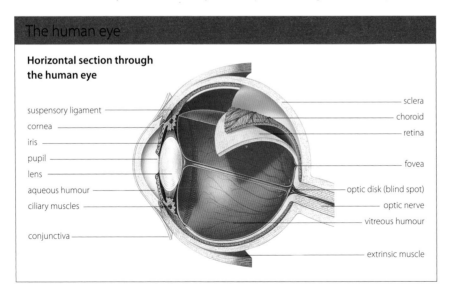

suspensory ligament

cornea

iris

pupil

lens

aqueous humour

ciliary muscles

conjunctiva

sclera

choroid

retina

fovea

optic disk (blind spot)

optic nerve

vitreous humour

extrinsic muscle

Pupil reflex

A nervous-system response called 'pupil reflex' controls the size of the pupils and thus the amount of light entering the eyeball. If there is too much light (A) then the circular pupillary muscles contract (1) and the radial fibres (2)

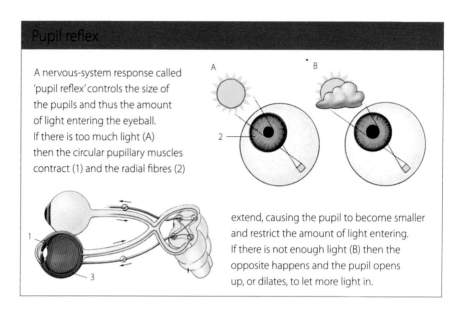

extend, causing the pupil to become smaller and restrict the amount of light entering. If there is not enough light (B) then the opposite happens and the pupil opens up, or dilates, to let more light in.

needed before your eyes become optimally primed for astronomy. Try this out sometime soon. Resist the urge to use a torch in the dark and give your eyes a chance to adjust and you will be amazed how much you can see. Be warned, though – exposure to bright lights can instantly destroy your dark adaptation, leaving you with another hour to wait before you get it back again. That is one of the many reasons why astronomers tend to get a bit tetchy around lights! There will be occasions when you will need a little light and the lower energy of red light means this is the best colour torch to get. Red bicycle lights can be a little too bright, so find your nearest astronomical dealer and get hold of a proper red torch designed for astronomers.

Dark adaptation is not the only issue that you will need to be aware of. There is another little 'design feature' of the eye ready to trip up the keen but unwary astronomer. It turns out that not only do our light-sensitive detectors have different purposes, but they are also arranged in a very specific pattern. If you focus your attention on an object and look straight at it, most of the light hits a part of your retina called the macula. It is here that the cones are more numerous and densely populated. There are around 6 million cones in one human eye and they are less sensitive than the rods. Surrounding the macula are around 120 million rods, which are much more sensitive but are pretty rubbish at detecting colour.

If you take a look through a telescope at a planet all is well. Planets are bright with plenty of light, most if not all of which will hit your cones and you will be able to see delicate colours in the belts of Jupiter or easily pick out the red colour of Mars. But point the telescope at a fainter galaxy or gas cloud and you will be disappointed to see a grey-green smudge of light! Unfortunately, you will never see the glorious colours in these objects that you see in wonderful photographs, simply because neither your rods nor your cones are sensitive enough. However, you can improve the detail that you can see by

► *The Blinking Nebula in Cygnus nicely demonstrates averted vision.*

sending the light from the object on to the more sensitive rods. Fortunately, you do not need to head off to your nearest hospital for an operation to achieve this – instead there is a great little technique called *averted vision.* All you do is look slightly to one side of the object you are studying and, as if by magic, it pops into view in greater detail. The trick here is not to move your gaze back on to it again immediately, but practice will soon turn you into an expert. Try it now – focus your eyes on a blank part of this page but try and look at some words out of the corner of your eye! There is a wonderful little object called the 'Blinking Nebula', in the constellation Cygnus, which we can observe by making use of this effect. It is the remnant of a star that died millions of years ago which can still be seen as a faint misty nebula surrounding the core of a dead star. When you look at it using averted vision it does quite a wonderful thing. Look straight at it first to see the faint stellar corpse in the middle, then look to one side to allow the light to fall on to your rods and the faint nebulosity will pop into view while the star seems to vanish. Alternating your gaze will make it appear to blink on and off at you.

Looking at the sky with your eyes or even with optical aid means you are looking at the Universe in a particular type of light we call *visible light*, yet visible light is just a tiny part of the electromagnetic spectrum. The idea of a larger spectrum of 'light' beyond that which we can see with the eye is perhaps a little easier to visualize if you think about a rainbow. When sunlight passes through droplets of water in the atmosphere it gets broken up into its individual colours from red through orange, yellow, green, blue, indigo and finally violet, and we can see this in the beautiful rainbows on a rainy day. The thing that separates one colour from the next is its wavelength. We can think of light as ripples on a pond where the distance from one wave crest to the next is the wavelength. Light at the red end of the rainbow has a wavelength of 650 nanometres (or 0.00065 millimetres), whereas violet light has a shorter wavelength of 400 nm (or 0.0004 mm).

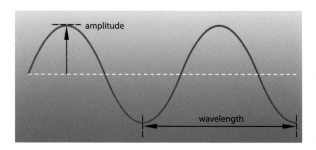

◄ *Light can be thought of as a wave, much like those seen on the sea. Amplitude describes the height of the wave and wavelength the distance between two successive peaks or troughs.*

It is easy now to visualize that there might be light or radiation at opposite ends of the rainbow which is invisible to our eyes, and in fact, as I've already mentioned, visible light makes up only a tiny portion of the much greater electromagnetic spectrum, with wavelength being the factor that differentiates between them all. Extending out beyond the violet end of the spectrum is ultraviolet radiation followed by X-rays and finally gamma-rays, and beyond the red end are infrared, microwaves and lastly radio waves. To get a full understanding of the Universe we need to study the sky in all these different wavelengths, but one challenge facing astronomers is that a high proportion get blocked by our atmosphere. Gamma-rays, X-rays and the majority of ultraviolet radiation are blocked by the atmosphere, as are the vast proportion of infrared radiation and the longer-wavelength end of the radio waves. To solve this problem and to allow observations in these wavelengths astronomers must put telescopes up in orbit high above the blocking effects of the atmosphere. This is all-important to get a fuller understanding of the mechanics of the Universe, otherwise we are missing out on crucial information hidden in the other wavelengths. It is a bit like just listening to the string section of an orchestra where you would only hear their sound, but to get a full appreciation for the whole piece of music you must listen to all sections. The Universe is the same and we must tune in to all sections of the electromagnetic spectrum in order to fully capture the information hidden in starlight. For amateur astronomy, though, we can only hope to focus attention on the messages in light hitting the ground so must be content with visible light, a little of the ultraviolet, infrared and radio waves.

Understanding how light and our eyes work is just the first step in getting started in astronomy, but having a red torch, letting your eyes adapt to the dark and using averted

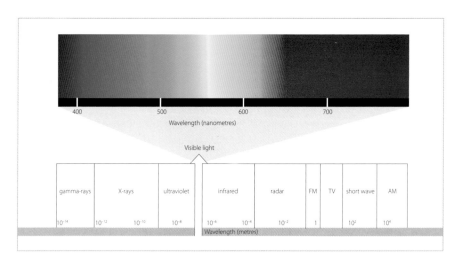

▲ *Studying the Universe means looking at it not only in visible light but in all wavelengths of the electromagnetic spectrum, from gamma-rays to radio waves. The spectrum above shows that visible light is only a tiny portion, so restricting our view means we are not getting the full picture.*

▲ *Sunrise and sunset are among the most basic astronomical observations anyone can make. This image is of Stonehenge, Wiltshire, at sunrise.*

vision can greatly aid even naked-eye astronomy. The next step is to start looking at the sky and understand how it moves, which is something you already know about without even realizing it. Since your childhood you have been aware that the Sun rises in the east and sets in the west. Before the days of reasoning it was thought that the gods powered the movement of the Sun across the sky, when in reality it is something a little less ethereal.

Our entire Solar System, including the Sun and planets, formed out of a vast swirling cloud of gas and dust known as a nebula. Over many millions of years, gravity took hold and started to cause the cloud to collapse into regions of higher density, which ultimately formed the Sun and planets. Those objects all retained the original motion of the cloud as it collapsed, and although other events have caused minor changes, the rotation still exists today. It is the rotation of the Earth that it inherited from the nebula which results in the appearance of the Sun rising and setting in the way we are so familiar with. So you already know that the Earth spins on its axis once every day. In reality it takes a little less than 24 hours for the Earth to spin once on its axis – 23 hours 56 minutes and 4 seconds to be precise – which is known as a *sidereal day* or the day with reference to the stars.

We humans quite like to take the easy route so our clocks and watches use 24 hours as a day – however, the slight discrepancy of 3 minutes 56 seconds has an effect that is quite

▲ *The Eagle Nebula, photographed by the Hubble Space Telescope, is a stunning example of a star-forming region, 5,700 light years away.*

important to the astronomer. You might think that you could look at the sky night after night at exactly the same time and see exactly the same view – wrong! The slight time difference between the rotation of the Earth and the day on our watches means you would have to look at the sky 3 minutes 56 seconds earlier each night to see the same sky. As the days turn into weeks and the weeks turn into months, we slowly see a different set of constellations in the sky. Look at the sky in June and you will see a completely different set of objects than if you look again at the same time in December.

Day and night

The Sun appears to rise in the east, reach its highest point at noon, and then set in the west, to be followed by night. In reality, it is not the Sun that is moving but the Earth rotating from west to east. The moment when the Sun's upper limb first appears above the horizon is termed sunrise; the moment when the Sun's upper limb disappears below the horizon is sunset. At the summer solstice in the northern hemisphere (20 or 21 June), the Arctic has total daylight and the Antarctic total darkness. The opposite occurs at the winter solstice (21 or 22 December). At the Equator, the length of day and night are almost equal all year.

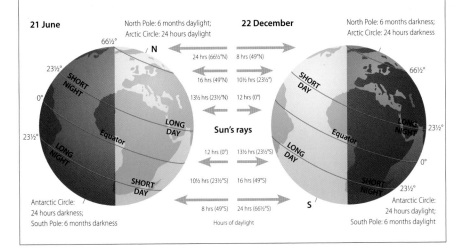

It is an interesting aside to note that as the Earth travels around the Sun, it is the tilt of the Earth on its axis which gives rise to the seasons, not the proximity to the Sun. You would think that Earth is closer to the Sun in June/July giving rise to the warmer seasons, but do not forget that the southern hemisphere experiences its coldest weather at this time. In reality the northern hemisphere of the Earth is pointing towards the Sun during the summer months, giving us the most intense solar radiation and the warmer weather, while the southern hemisphere is pointing away from the Sun. Conversely, in the northern winter months around December and January the northern hemisphere is pointing away from the Sun, getting less intense solar radiation so we experience cooler weather, which is when the southern hemisphere is basking in summer.

The constellations you can see in the sky vary too depending on where you are in the world. The Earth is a sphere (it is actually more like a ball which has been squashed very slightly into a shape known as an oblate spheroid) upon which we all live. Our location on the Earth is defined by a co-ordinate system using latitude and longitude. The latitude co-ordinate explains position north or south of the Equator (the imaginary line which runs around the middle) and longitude defines position east or west of another imaginary and arbitrarily positioned line called the Greenwich Meridian, which not surprisingly passes through Greenwich in London.

Seasons occur because the Earth's axis is tilted at an angle of approximately 23½°. When the northern hemisphere is tilted to a maximum extent towards the Sun, on 20 or 21 June, the Sun is overhead at the Tropic of Cancer (latitude 23½° North). This is midsummer, or the summer solstice, in the northern hemisphere.

On 22 or 23 September, the Sun is overhead at the Equator, and day and night are of equal length throughout the world. This is the autumnal equinox in the northern hemisphere.

On 21 or 22 December, the Sun is overhead at the Tropic of Capricorn (23½° South), the winter solstice in the northern hemisphere. The overhead Sun then tracks north until, on 20 or 21 March, it is overhead at the Equator. This is the spring (vernal) equinox in the northern hemisphere.

In the southern hemisphere, the seasons are the reverse of those in the north.

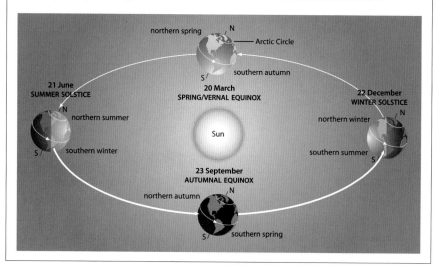

Those people living in Europe will see one set of constellations throughout the year while those living in South America will see another set of constellations, some of which will be the same, others only visible from the different locations. Just as I started writing this book I was on holiday in Turkey, which has a lower latitude than the UK, and from there I could see mostly the same constellations but they were a little higher in the sky. In the southern part of the sky I could also see a few stars that I couldn't normally see from my home in England.

Just like the Earth, the sky has its own co-ordinate system based on the idea of latitude and longitude. If you imagine the entire sky as a vast crystal sphere with the Earth sitting at its centre then it is also easy to imagine Earth's Equator being extended out to run around the sphere too. We call the imaginary sphere the *celestial sphere* and the imaginary equator on the sky is the *celestial equator*. The astronomical equivalent of latitude is called *declination* and is based on the distance north or south of the celestial equator. Objects that lie on the celestial equator are said to have a declination of 0° (zero). We can also extend the position of

▶ *The popular asterism of the Summer Triangle is seen against the Milky Way and marked by Deneb in Cygnus (top), Vega in Lyra (right) and Altair in Aquila (bottom).*

the poles on Earth on to the celestial sphere to give us the north and south celestial poles. These points in the sky have a declination of 90 degrees north (or +90°) and 90 degrees south (−90°). The position of the north and south celestial poles is where the rotational axis of the Earth points, which in the northern hemisphere currently lies very close to the faint star Polaris in the constellation Ursa Minor. There is no such equivalent star that marks the south celestial pole. Complicating matters a little more is the fact that the Earth is wobbling like a giant spinning top, so the position of the celestial poles will shift over many thousands of years – by the year 5200 AD, Deneb in Cygnus will become the northern Pole Star.

It is easy to understand that if you stood in a country on the Equator then the celestial equator would run over your head and the two celestial poles would sit on the northern and southern horizons. If you were to stand shivering at the North Pole then you would see the north celestial pole overhead and the celestial equator running around the horizon, with the south celestial pole out of view directly below your feet. From this you might have spotted a neat little fact: the height of the celestial pole is equal to the latitude from which you are looking at it, so for me, living in the UK which has a latitude of around 52°, the north celestial pole is 52° above the northern horizon. It also means that the celestial equator can be seen above the horizon due south but

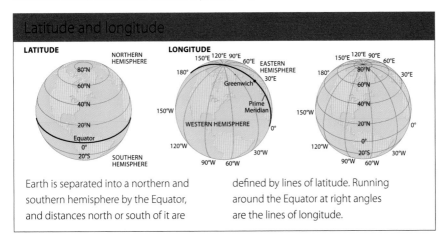

Latitude and longitude

Earth is separated into a northern and southern hemisphere by the Equator, and distances north or south of it are defined by lines of latitude. Running around the Equator at right angles are the lines of longitude.

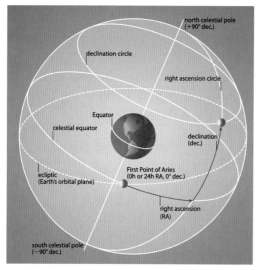

◀ *The celestial sphere is an imaginary sphere surrounding the Earth with its own set of co-ordinates: right ascension and declination.*

dips down below the horizon to the north. The highest point that the celestial equator reaches for me is around 38° when I look exactly south, so I can see some objects in the southern hemisphere of the sky. Understanding how much of the sky you can see will really help you when planning out an observing session. For most people in the UK, for example, throughout the year it is possible to see all objects in the northern hemisphere of the sky and objects down to around −38° in the sky's southern hemisphere. We look at how you can work this out for your location later in this chapter.

The celestial equivalent to longitude is *right ascension*. Unlike declination, which starts at the easily defined celestial equator, right ascension has no obvious starting point in the sky. Its starting point is instead linked to the movement of the Sun across the sky. Imagine it sitting at the centre of a giant sheet of paper with the paper slicing through its middle, with its northern hemisphere poking above the paper and the southern hemisphere below. The Earth would sit on the same sheet of paper at some distance away, travelling around the Sun in a giant ellipse and with the paper cutting the Earth in half, similar to the Sun. The plane that this sheet of paper represents is the plane of the Solar System and is known as the *ecliptic*.

From our viewpoint on Earth, it looks like the Sun travels along this ecliptic as it moves around the sky. In our analogy, the Earth doesn't sit in an upright fashion – instead it is tilted over at an angle of about 23.5°, so instead of the Earth's Equator running along the sheet of the paper, it too is tilted by about 23.5° when compared to the ecliptic. Both the ecliptic and the celestial equator are imaginary lines that run all the way around the sky, one tilted with respect to the other. The lines cross each other at two points, one of which used to lie in the constellation of Aries, hence its name 'the First Point of Aries'; however, due to the wobble of the Earth this point moves slowly over thousands of years and is now in the constellation of Pisces! It is from this point that the right ascension co-ordinate system starts, moving in an easterly direction around the sky. Unlike declination, which uses degrees as the unit of measure, right ascension uses hours, where 1 hour of right ascension is equal to about 15°. It starts at 0 hours at the First Point of Aries and runs easterly until a full circle is reached at 24 hours. Hours are used instead of degrees because the location of a star is generally determined by the time that it passes through the highest point in the sky as the Earth rotates.

The exact position of a star in the sky is defined by its right ascension and declination, and to allow for accurate positions to be plotted both co-ordinates are broken down further into minutes and seconds. In both cases, there are 60 seconds in a minute and 60 minutes in a degree or an hour. The bright star in Canis Major called Sirius has a right ascension of 6 hours 45 minutes and 46 seconds (RA 06h 45m 46s) and a declination of −16 degrees 43 minutes and 58 seconds (dec. −16° 43' 58"). If you look at a star chart you will see right ascension and declination depicted on the chart as a grid, just as you would see latitude and longitude on a map of the world.

Star charts show much more than just objects and their co-ordinates – you will also find the stars are shown as different sized dots, with smaller ones representing fainter stars and larger dots showing the brighter stars. The brightness of a star is referred to as its magnitude, or more accurately its *apparent magnitude*. The faintest stars visible to the naked eye are magnitude 6, while Sirius, the brightest star in the sky, is so bright that it has a negative value of −1.4. It is important to stress that I am referring to apparent magnitude, which describes how bright an object is in the sky. This is different to the *absolute magnitude*, which goes some way in trying to define how bright an object is in comparison with other objects. It defines how bright an object would be if it were at a distance from Earth of 10 parsecs, where 1 parsec is equal to 3.26 light years. The *light year* is the distance light can travel in one year, travelling at about 300,000 km/sec, but the parsec is a little more complicated to understand, although there is a great little experiment you can do now to help you understand it. Extend your arm and point one finger up to the sky – now shut one eye and, through the other, look to see where the finger appears with reference to background objects. Now shut that eye and open the other, and you will notice your finger has magically shifted. This apparent shift of your finger is the result of looking at it from different positions – in other words, through your two eyes. If you really wanted, you could now calculate the length of your arm by knowing the distance between your eyes and by measuring the tiny angular shift of your finger!

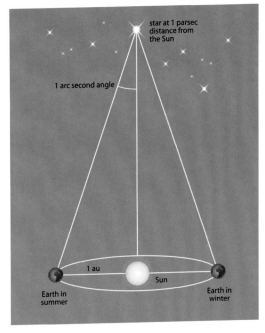

We can do similar experiments in astronomy by looking at stars from the extremities of the orbit of Earth and looking at their tiny apparent shifts. This is all relevant in the discussion of the parsec because 1 parsec is equal to the distance that a star exhibits an angular shift, known as *parallax*, of 1 arc second or 1/3,600 of a degree, which is 1,800 times smaller than the diameter of the full Moon! Remember that absolute magnitude defines an object's brightness at a distance of 10 parsecs, so by doing this for all objects we can get a feel for how bright they really are. Not only do star charts give you a good

▶ *One parsec is the distance that a star must be for it to exhibit a parallax shift of 1 arc second.*

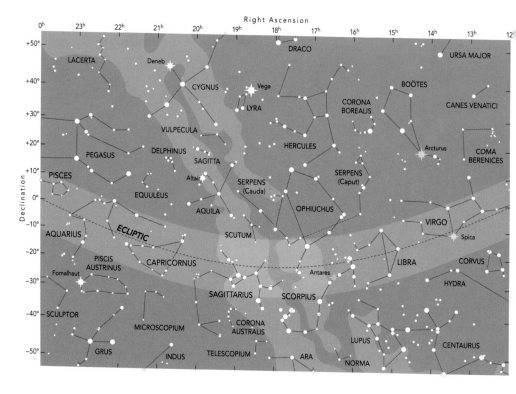

▲ *Star chart showing right ascension (RA) and declination (dec.). Like places on Earth, objects in the sky have their position described by a grid system.*

graphical representation of stellar brightness but you will also find other objects like star clusters, galaxies and nebulae on the charts. However, the things you won't find printed are the Sun, Moon and planets because they all move with respect to each other. Stars do move their position, but it takes thousands of years for that motion to be easily detected so star charts are only updated every 50 years or so.

There is another commonly used co-ordinate system used in astronomy which is not depicted on star charts, and this uses a terrestrial system based on altitude and azimuth. Instead of describing an object's position from the celestial equator or the First Point of Aries, this one looks at the position of an object from your observing location based on the horizon and the direction of due north. It makes it a lot easier for someone to understand roughly where to look in the sky to find something, but it does mean that, as objects move across the sky, their altitude and azimuth co-ordinates change. The term *altitude* defines the height above the horizon, from 0° at the horizon up to the point overhead known as the zenith, which is 90°. *Azimuth*, on the other hand, measures the angle around the horizon from due north in an easterly direction. The northern point on the compass would have an azimuth of 0°, due east is 90°, south is 180° and west is 270°. Using Sirius again as the example, as it rises in the south-eastern sky it might have an azimuth of 130° and an altitude of 7°. As the night

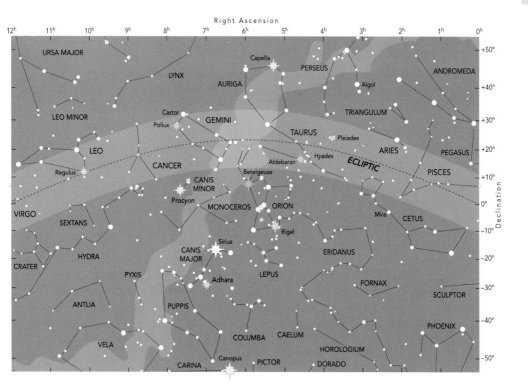

Right Ascension

progresses and it climbs higher in the sky, its co-ordinates will change to an azimuth of 180°
when due south and an altitude of 20°.

In practical terms, a combination of right ascension and declination along with altitude
and azimuth are used by amateur astronomers when trying to hone in on target objects.
One of the first things to do when you want to find an object is to see when it is above the
horizon. That may seem like a silly statement, but you would be surprised at how many
people I have spoken to over the years who just did not realize that some things can only
be seen at certain times of the year. (Mind you, I have also had people seem surprised that

The light year
A quick side note here to explain a *light year*. Light is the fastest thing in the Universe
and travels at 300,000 km/sec. At that speed, light can travel 9.5 million million km in
one year. We use this distance as a scale in astronomy so that 1 light year equates to
9.5 million million km. The nearest galaxy to our own, the Andromeda Galaxy, is
just over 2.3 million light years away. That's a whole lot easier to say, and deal with,
than 21.8 million million million km – and that is the nearest! The most distant object
discovered to date is a galaxy 13.4 billion light years away. Needless to say, galaxies are
a long way away!

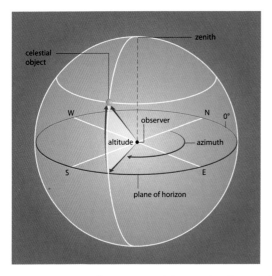

zenith

celestial
object

W

observer

N   0°

altitude

azimuth

S

E

plane of horizon

◀ *The altitude of an astronomical
object is its height above the horizon
measured in degrees where the
horizon is 0° and overhead is 90°.*

I could not show them anything because it
was raining – 'Why isn't the telescope working?') It is because we live on a big ball that
allows us to look out in different directions
as it spins and as we orbit the Sun. From
here in the UK, for example, it is no good
looking for the constellation Orion in May
because it is only above the horizon in the
daytime.

With experience you will know what
you can see at different times of the night
and at different times of the year, but for now there are a few useful hints and tips I can share
with you. I have already explained that Polaris sits very close to the north celestial pole,
which is where the Earth's axis of rotation points in the northern hemisphere. Looking north
you can pinpoint Polaris, as it will be the same number of degrees above the horizon as your
latitude. Estimating angular distances like this on the sky is quite easy if you use your hand!
An outstretched hand at arm's length measures about 20° from thumb to little finger, while
a clenched fist equals about 10°. You can gauge smaller measurements from the width of
the three middle fingers, which are equivalent to 5°, or the width of one finger which is equal
to about 1°.

Using these methods, you can estimate where Polaris should be in the sky and locate
it at the tip of the tail of Ursa Minor, the Little Bear. If you look at it over a period of hours
you will notice that it does not seem to move. Look further south, on the other hand, and
the stars seem to move quite a bit quicker, with the fastest being found around the
celestial equator. What you will notice, if you look at the sky over a few nights, is that Polaris
is always in the same position whenever you look, whereas stars and constellations further
away rise and set. There is an area of the sky specific to your latitude where any stars will
circle the celestial pole but will never set, even during the day. These are called *circumpolar
stars* and, from the UK, all of the stars in the group known as the Plough fall into this
category. When planning observing programmes, it is useful to know which stars are
circumpolar and this can be done with a really simple calculation. All you need to do is
subtract your latitude from 90! My latitude is about 52° so subtracting that from 90 will
give 38, so any star with a declination of 38° or more will be circumpolar from my location.
Anything with a declination less than that will set at some point.

The best time to see any objects in the night sky is when they are at their highest,
which means they pass across an imaginary line that runs from the northern point on the
horizon, up through Polaris, directly overhead through the zenith and down to the point
where the horizon is due south. When stars pass this line they are said to culminate, and at

this point their light is passing through the least amount of gas in our atmosphere, giving us the best views. Circumpolar stars pass this point on two occasions: a lower culmination when they pass lower than Polaris and an upper culmination when they pass above it. The best time to look at the circumpolar objects is at upper culmination.

For the rest of your planning activities there are a number of options. If you do not have access to smart phones or computers then the simplest way to start is with a Philip's planisphere. These clever little devices are maps of the sky consisting of two plastic disks joined at the centre and able to rotate against each other. The bottom disk has a map of the sky with stars, co-ordinate lines, celestial equator and ecliptic all printed on it and the days of the year printed around the outside. The upper disk is opaque except for an oval window which allows you to see a portion of the star chart underneath. Around the edge of this disk are the hours of the day and to set it up is simply a matter of matching the current date against the current time. This will show you which constellations are visible in the sky at that time of day. Planispheres only cost a few pounds but are a worthwhile investment. Having worked out which constellations are visible, it is easy to determine which planets can be seen from tables on the back of the planisphere or which galaxies and clusters can be seen from more detailed star charts.

It is worth planning your observing so that you start with objects over in the west, which are heading lower in the sky as they move towards setting. The further west and lower they get, the worse the view will become. Once you have these objects identified, move across to the objects due south, which will be optimally placed for observation. Something else to consider is the way that the atmosphere cools down in the early hours before dawn. This means it becomes more stable and there is less turbulent air for light to travel through, so highly magnified views are best left until the early hours. There are some great websites on the internet and free software available to help you plan your observing. Search for 'planetarium software' or 'astronomical observation planning' in an internet search engine and you will find plenty to choose from.

Where and when you choose to observe will depend largely on yourself. Personally, I find it much more rewarding to observe with groups of friends, but many people are more than happy under a night sky on their own with their telescope quietly exploring the Universe.

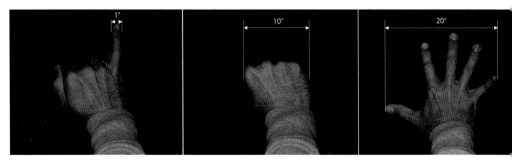

▲ *Hand measurements: at arm's length, the little finger represents an angular measurement on the sky of 1°, a clenched fist is equal to about 10°, and an outstretched hand is around 20°.*

▲ *A planisphere is a wonderful gizmo that will help you find your way around the night sky.*

Most towns and cities, even some villages, have a local astronomy society and these are great places to go to find like-minded people, some of whom will eventually become good friends, and you will get lots of advice and practical experience under the watchful eye of experienced astronomers. Many of them organize observing sessions – some of them even invite the general public along to get a taste for the subject. I find these great social occasions and get a great deal of enjoyment out of them.

Even if you cannot find a local society, you may want to make a trip to one of the many star parties that are organized in countries around the world. Star parties are really good fun and, as their name suggests, are events focused around astronomy. They usually follow the format of taking over part or all of a camp site for the event where astronomers from near and far come along, camp in tents or stay in caravans, and set up their equipment in one massive observing session. I am lucky enough to live in Norfolk and have two great star parties each year: the Kelling Heath star parties, one held around the Spring Equinox and the other around the Autumnal Equinox. Generally, these events last for a few days and are at locations where the skies are very dark. You might find yourself unlucky and have a few days of cloud, but, regardless, there is still a great deal of enjoyment in chatting to people about their equipment and experiences. On the nights that are clear, it is a surreal experience to wander around a camp site in the dead of night to hear the whirr of motors and see the gentle glow of tiny little LED lights on equipment as telescopes of all shapes and sizes peer into the depths of space. It is a great way of immersing yourself in astronomy for a few days with like-minded individuals. You will often find trade stands there too, where good deals can be struck on telescopes and accessories, so it is well worth making the effort to go along. Other great star parties in the UK take place at Kielder Forest and in the Peak District, and over in the United States there is possibly one of the largest parties, held in Arizona.

Wherever you observe from, you will need to wait for a clear night, preferably without the Moon as its light can limit the number of stars you will see, and get away from artificial lighting if you can. You might find yourself waiting quite some time for a decent clear night and as you progress in astronomy you will notice that clear nights are not always actually good nights. Studying the Universe means looking through almost 100 km of gas within which are the wonderful weather systems we all know and 'love'. There will be nights when you poke your head out of the door to see stars only to find that on closer inspection there is a thin layer of cloud. These nights can be great for planetary observing but fainter galaxies and nebulosity can be lost. Equally, there will be nights of unprecedented clarity where really faint objects can be seen but the instability of the atmosphere means fine levels of detail are lost in the bubbly turbulence.

There are two ways that astronomers describe the conditions in the sky and you will most certainly come across these. The first and most obvious is described as *seeing*, which simply explains how stable the atmosphere is. You can see the effect of bad seeing by looking at stars low near the horizon that seem to twinkle wildly. The worse the seeing, the more twinkly they appear, which is caused by the movement of gas in the atmosphere that disturbs the incoming beams of light from objects in space. It can be the clearest of nights with an inky black sky but the seeing can still be awful. Trying to study planets, the Moon or close binary stars on nights like these can be really poor if not impossible. Through a telescope the image will be bubbling around and detail will be really hard to see. But despite the bubbling, boiling images of stars and planets, these nights are great for getting out and learning to find your way around. You may well hear people talk about the Antoniadi scale when talking of seeing conditions, which is a really useful way of quantifying the seeing. The scale was devised by Greek astronomer Eugene Antoniadi, who was a prolific observer of Mars, and is based on a five-point system using Roman numerals, with these original definitions:

I   Perfect seeing, without a quiver.
II   Slight quivering of the image with moments of calm lasting several seconds.
III   Moderate seeing with larger air tremors that blur the image.
IV   Poor seeing, constant troublesome undulations of the image.
V   Very bad seeing, hardly stable enough to allow a rough sketch to be made.

The other phrase used to explain the conditions is *transparency*, which refers to the clearness or clarity of the sky. This is generally in relation to atmospheric pollutants and dust suspended in the atmosphere, so on some nights it can be clear but 'murky' and fainter objects are not easily visible. Rain is actually a good thing for astronomers because it clears all the rubbish out of the atmosphere, so skies after a rainfall can have excellent transparency with really faint objects being visible. Keep an eye on the weather and look with a critical eye to get the best out of the conditions: if there's good seeing and poor transparency then stick to planets, lunar observing and binary stars; if there's good transparency *and* poor seeing then aim for faint diffuse objects like galaxies and nebulae; but if there's good seeing and good transparency then have a field day, as these nights do not happen often enough! Be aware of the wind too, as on a windy night astronomers without the protection of an observatory will find their telescope getting battered around in the wind, making high magnifications unrealistic.

I have enjoyed some of the most stable skies during the early hours before the onset of twilight from the rising Sun. The effect of heating from the Sun causes the atmosphere to move around, resulting in turbulence and bad seeing – but as night falls and the Sun drops below the horizon, the Earth will eventually stop radiating heat up into the atmosphere and when it does, usually after midnight, the atmosphere finally becomes stable, and it is at these times that the seeing can be the best. I am rubbish at getting up in the early hours so just tend to stay up all night and wait for the early hours after midnight when most lights will have been switched off giving darker skies, the atmosphere will be calm and the viewing can be amazing.

I made a point earlier about getting away from man-made lighting, and while this is important it is not essential unless you are in the centre of a large city, like London. I spent the majority of my first 10 years looking at the sky from my parents' house on the outskirts of Norwich, which is a moderate-sized city – it just makes it a little more challenging and you will not be able to see the night sky at its best.

We are now nearly ready to get out under the stars, but it is really important that you are physically prepared for the night's observing. If you, like me, live in a part of the world that experiences cool, even cold, nights then it will come as no surprise that one of the biggest challenges facing us is keeping warm. Unfortunately, the best views are achieved during some of the coldest nights of the year, and with hours of standing around in the elements it is essential for your enjoyment, comfort and even health to be prepared. I have tried numerous different ways to keep warm but have found an approach that seems to work for me, and given that you will be spending some of your hard-earned cash on a telescope, it is well worth investing in some decent clothing to keep you warm.

One of the usual traps people seem to fall into when preparing for a night out under the stars is to wear lots of layers. The concept of layering clothing is fine if you are moving around. The air gaps between all the layers trap the heat generated by your body during movement – but astronomy is not the most active of pursuits. Long periods of time spent standing around demand insulation instead of just layers. Get yourself some thermal underwear, thermal socks too, and another layer like a fleece top and fleece-lined windproof trousers, finished off with a good, thick, insulated jacket. The jacket is vitally important as it keeps your core body temperature up, so aim for something filled with 'down' rather than thick fleeces. Jackets are listed with a specification called 'fill power', which defines volume of down

▲ *Living near built-up areas need not put an end to astronomy. You just need to think a little more about how you are going to do it and what you are going to look at.*

when compressed under a certain weight, and mine, which keeps me toasty warm even on the coldest of nights, is 700 fill power. Make sure to cover your head too, as that is a place where lots of heat is lost. Your feet also need to be well covered, so thick woollen socks and boots with a good sole will ensure heat is not lost to the ground. If you do find your hands getting cold (as they are more at risk while you fiddle with equipment) then a really neat trick is to swing your arms back and forth for a good few minutes, which forces blood into the hands through centrifugal force. It's best to keep your hands lower than your heart as this minimizes stresses on it. Surprisingly, it works and lasts for quite a while. Gloves are still a very worthwhile investment and mine have metallic pads in the tips of thumb and forefinger so I can still operate smartphones and tablet computers.

If you are planning a long or even an all-night observing session then you should also not forget food and drink. It is very easy to be outside in the hours of darkness and not realize that, because you are perhaps not used to being up so late, your body will need fuel. Bananas are a great source of slow-release energy to help you keep awake, and plenty of water is essential to ensure you do not get dehydrated in the cold dry night air. You would be surprised how refreshing water can be when observing. But for me, a night observing is not complete without a bacon sandwich at some ridiculous time of night – plenty of protein and warming, too. I am probably trying to justify this, but it is fair to say that a bacon sandwich is quite a common sight at observing sessions!

So, you are all prepared now and it's time to get outside and explore the Universe. Easier said than done because you actually have to find the objects you want to look at, but whether you are using a telescope or observing with the naked eye there is a great little technique called *star hopping* that will help you no end. As its name suggests, star hopping involves hopping from one star to another until you find your chosen target. A great example of using this technique is to find the Andromeda Galaxy, not surprisingly in the constellation of Andromeda. Using the star-hopping method to find it means first locating the Square of Pegasus, which is nicely placed in the southern sky during October from the UK. The stars of the Square are all of similar brightness and easy to see with the naked eye, as is the shape which forms the body of the winged horse. The next step is to identify the star at the north-eastern corner of the Square called Alpheratz, and from there move further to the east, away from the Square by about 7°, which is a little less than the width of your fist at arm's length. Here you will find a red star called Delta Andromedae. Moving a little further east by about the same distance and forming a very shallow triangle with the first two stars is Mirach, another red-coloured star which is a little brighter than Delta Andromedae. A change of direction is needed now, so imagine taking a right turn when you reach Mirach and heading north. After a distance of just 3° (the width of three fingers at arm's length) you will see a fainter white-coloured star called Mu Andromedae, and further north for the same distance will take you to a faint fuzzy patch of light, the Andromeda Galaxy. It may not look too impressive at first glance, but it is one of the most distant objects visible to the human eye at a whopping 2.3 million light years. That means the light has taken 2.3 million years to get here, travelling at 300,000 km/sec! Using star hopping in this way is all about finding something bright and easy to identify, and then gauging brightnesses of stars you are hopping to and imagining lines and shapes between the stars.

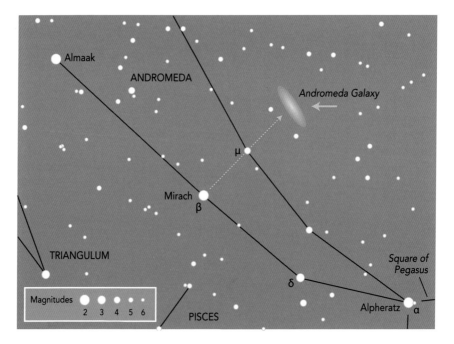

▲ *Star-hopping route to the Andromeda Galaxy from the Great Square of Pegasus.*

▲ *The Andromeda Galaxy is a great first deep-sky target for beginners.*

For star hopping with a telescope I find it really helpful to make up a little plastic guide. Line up your finder telescope (more on these in Chapter 5) on something like the Pleiades or another area of the sky that is easy to find with plenty of bright stars. As you look through the finder, make a mental note of which stars you can see on one edge of the field of view. Now take a piece of clear plastic and overlay it on a star chart of the same area. Using a permanent marker, make a tiny mark on the plastic to represent the edge of the field of view. Now do the same on the opposite side and to the top and bottom. You will now have four dots representing how much sky you can see through the finder. Join these dots into a circle (you could try and find something of roughly the same size to help make a neater job of this). The circle will allow you to represent on the star chart the stars you can see in the sky through the finder, and to use it simply line up your telescope on your chosen starting point then star hop the plastic disk to the next hop with some easily recognizable star patterns. Nudge the telescope along to find the same pattern before repeating again, until you have hopped your way to the target. Using this approach makes telescopic star hopping much easier, particularly as most telescopes will represent the sky upside down or back to front! There are a few well-used star-hopping routes across the sky and we will look at some of these in the next chapter, but do not be afraid to experiment and make up your own routes.

For now, get outside, spend some time letting your eyes adjust to the darkness and start hopping around the sky. Do not be scared just to look and be amazed – I sometimes find that's the most incredible part of astronomy: no complications, no equipment, just me and the Universe. Now that you have got to the end of this first chapter, you will have a great grasp of the basics so let's get out under the sky together, put it all into practice in Chapter 2 and start to find some celestial wonders.

MARK'S STARGAZING QUICK-START GUIDE

Tip 1   Buy a red torch

It takes between 40 minutes and an hour for your eyes to become fully adapted to seeing in the dark, but even astronomers need a little light sometimes, perhaps to read a chart or attend to equipment. Any exposure to bright lights will instantly ruin this dark adaptation but there is a solution. Red light is the least energetic of the visible spectrum and so is ideal, as it will not affect your ability to see in the dark. Bright red lights can still be problematic, though, and may still reduce your dark adaptation so it is best to resist using a rear bicycle light or those designed for walkers. A better idea is to buy a purpose-built red torch, just for astronomers, and you can find suppliers in any astronomy magazine.

Tip 2   Buy a planisphere or download an app

Along with a red torch, the other item that most astronomers have is a planisphere. These are very versatile star charts made of plastic and can be bought from most bookshops or online. By setting the date and time on the rotating disks they will show you the night sky from your location and time. A Philip's planisphere will even show you how you can locate the planets. For those who are more technologically minded, an alternative is to download a smartphone app. There are hundreds of these available for the different platforms – by holding them up to the sky, they will simulate the view of the sky in the direction you are pointing and tell you which objects are there.

Tip 3   Subscribe to an astronomy magazine

There is no better way to keep up to date with what's going on in the world of astronomy than subscribing to an astronomy magazine. Most countries have at least one or two good ones dedicated to the subject. Inside the covers, you will find news, equipment reviews, classified adverts and even monthly sky charts. Be warned, though – the monthly sky charts will be specific to the country of origin of the magazine, so while there will be loads of really great articles to read, the observational information may not be relevant to you. *Astronomy Now* is a great beginner's magazine in the UK, and for the more advanced amateur then *Sky & Telescope*, which is published in the United States, has some great in-depth articles. However, remember that the times and details of objects on view may not be relevant to readers outside the US.

Tip 4 Join your local astronomical society

Whether you intend to stick with casual stargazing or want to get more involved, a great and very enjoyable way to enhance your new hobby is to seek out your local astronomical society. They are excellent places to go for advice and help, and eventually you will find that observing with your newfound friends makes your observing sessions much more enjoyable. Not only will you make friends but you may also have the opportunity to try out different types of telescopes too, so you can make an informed decision before you buy your own. After a while, you may even find yourself getting involved in helping to run the group, perhaps assisting at public events, organizing observing sessions, joining the management committee or even giving lectures to newcomers yourself!

Tip 5 Get outside and start observing

Now to the most exciting bit, and that's to get outside and start learning your way around the night sky. You will be amazed at what you can see – those bright stars which aren't on your planisphere are probably planets and on your first night under the stars you may have already spotted satellites, meteorites and the odd passing aircraft. Time spent now familiarizing yourself with the sky will make your future enjoyment of the Universe much, much easier. Do not worry about buying a telescope yet as you will be amazed at what you can see with the naked eye. Chapter 2 of this book will help to guide you in the right direction. Then, after you have become familiar with the sky with the naked eye, you may want to move on to binoculars or a telescope to see things close-up and to reveal objects you couldn't otherwise see. If you do treat yourself to some binoculars or a telescope, you will need to invest in a more detailed star map or atlas to help you find your way around the thousands of faint stars you can now see.

Tip 6 Consider future equipment purchases

If stargazing is for you, then eventually you will be unable to wait any longer and will want to make that all-important purchase and buy yourself a pair of binoculars or even a telescope. But be sure to take your time and do not rush your decision – speak to people at your local club and see if you can look at a few different designs to find the right one for you. Chapter 3 will guide you through the experience of choosing your first telescope. Then, once you have purchased a telescope, consider other accessories like those listed in Chapter 5 – as your interest in astronomy develops, you will find yourself buying other equipment or even upgrading or changing your telescope.

chapter 2

WHAT YOU CAN SEE

ONE OF THE greatest challenges facing you as you start out in astronomy is finding your way around the night sky. The sight of a dark star-filled sky will fill you with wonder, awe and a huge chunk of dread as you realize that you have no idea where anything is! Chapter 1 has already set us in the right direction by explaining how the sky moves and how we navigate around it, in principle at least. The purpose of this chapter is to take that theory and turn it into real and practical stargazing greatness. Here there are four sections which show you what you can see in the night sky for each of the four seasons from mid-latitudes in the northern hemisphere, such as the UK, Canada, northern United States, northern European countries and southern Russia.

You will notice that the seasons are broken into months that may seem a little different to the ones you would usually associate with them. This is because I have used the astronomical definition of the seasons rather than the meteorological definition. According to astronomers, the seasons are centred upon the equinoxes and the solstices whereas meteorologists base them on average temperatures. You may already be familiar with the terms *equinox* and *solstice* (see panel on page 18), but it is appropriate to look at them now for clarity. We saw in Chapter 1 that the Earth is tilted over on its axis of rotation. This means that the celestial equator draws a circle around the sky which differs from the circle drawn by the Sun's apparent path, which is known as the ecliptic. The exact point in time when the Sun sits on the celestial equator is known as an equinox and so, on that day, areas all over the Earth will have equal hours of light and darkness. The equinoxes occur around 20 March and 22 September, and lead to our definition of spring (centred on the March or vernal equinox) and autumn (centred on the September or autumnal equinox). It is interesting to note that these terms of spring equinox and autumnal equinox are only relevant for the northern hemisphere, because the opposite is the case for the southern hemisphere, which experiences its spring equinox in September.

Summer and winter are defined by the solstices, which are the points when the Sun has reached its greatest angular distance in the sky from the celestial equator. Specifically

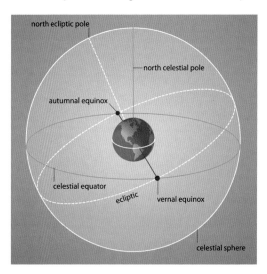

north ecliptic pole

north celestial pole

autumnal equinox

celestial equator

ecliptic

vernal equinox

celestial sphere

◀ *It is the tilt of the Earth that gives rise to the equinoxes and solstices.*

Sunrise and sunset

The times of sunrise and sunset vary not only with the time of year but also with your distance from the Equator (i.e. your latitude). The greater the latitude then the more varied will be the times of sunrise and sunset, but at two times each year they occur at the same local time everywhere on Earth.

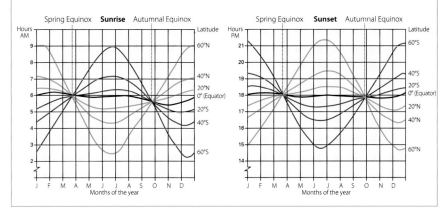

for the northern hemisphere, the Sun reaches its highest point in the sky around 21 June at the summer solstice, when we get the 'longest' days, and its lowest point in the sky around 21 December at the winter solstice, giving us our 'shortest' days. Again, the opposite is true for the southern hemisphere, which experiences its longest days around 21 December and its shortest days around 21 June.

The sky guides in this chapter show you how the sky looks for each month of the year but are grouped together into the seasons. The spring chart on page 37, for example, shows what the sky looks like on 15 March at 22:30, which will be the same around the middle of February but two hours later, and in the middle of April but two hours earlier. This does unfortunately mean that some of the charts show the sky in the hours just after midnight, but this is so that all the charts show the sky when it is properly dark. Along with the sky charts for each season you will find common star-hopping routes described to help you work your way around the sky, and constellation close-ups for the major constellations on view. I am unable to show you where the planets are because they move, but either a Philip's planisphere or the multitude of smartphone apps or computer software can help you locate them.

As we navigate around the sky together, I will often refer to distances between objects in degrees (°). This may seem a little alien to you now, but it is really quite simple and you have already come across it in the section explaining altitude and azimuth (see page 22). If you imagine standing facing north and then turning your head to look in the direction your right shoulder is pointing, then your head will have moved through 90°. If you were like an owl and could turn your head even further to look behind you, then you would have turned through 180°. Even further round to look in the direction of your left shoulder would take

Greek alphabet

α	alpha	ι	iota	ρ	rho
β	beta	κ	kappa	σ	sigma
γ	gamma	λ	lambda	τ	tau
δ	delta	μ	mu	υ	upsilon
ε	epsilon	ν	nu	φ	phi
ζ	zeta	ξ	xi	χ	chi
η	eta	ο	omicron	ψ	psi
θ	theta	π	pi	ω	omega

you through 270°, and then back to the north and you have travelled a full 360°. The distance between the horizon and the point over your head is 90°, so you can see that big distances are easy to visualize; smaller distances are a little harder – the full Moon, for example, is only half a degree across. Fortunately, you can use your hand and fingers as a guide to distances in the sky, as we saw in Chapter 1. It's really fortunate that people with bigger hands tend to have longer arms and those with shorter arms tend to have smaller hands, so this works with everyone. I refer back to these a lot when I am guiding you around the sky so don't forget you can look back at the guide in Chapter 1 as we work our way around the sky.

You will notice that the stars on the charts are depicted as dots of varying size, and again we saw this in Chapter 1. This simply gives you a guide to how bright the stars will appear in the sky, with the larger dots representing the brighter ones and the smaller dots the fainter ones. The brighter stars in the sky are all given real names that often sound peculiar, such as Betelguese, Sirius and Regulus, but they are also assigned a letter of the Greek alphabet, called its 'Bayer designation'. The brightest star in a constellation is usually given the designation of alpha but there are a few exceptions to this, such as Alpha Orionis, otherwise known as Betelgeuse, which is actually the second brightest star in Orion. It is a variable star that has changed in brightness since it was given its designation, but the general rule of thumb is that alpha is the brightest, and as you progress through the Greek alphabet, the stars get fainter and fainter. In astronomy, though, the brighter stars are generally referred to by their name and only the fainter ones by their Bayer designation. A mixture of these is used in these charts and descriptions.

The stars that you can see in the sky are all members of constellations that are human inventions to group stars together, making it easier to articulate where they are. The constellations have origins in many different cultures but the names in use today are agreed upon by the International Astronomical Union. There are 88 constellations, which vary in size and prominence, and they not only represent the bright stars making up the shapes like Ursa Major, the Great Bear, but the multitude of fainter stars and other objects which are also said to lie within the constellation. It is more proper to say that a constellation is an area of the celestial sphere, within which are stars, galaxies and a whole host of other objects. For your reference, a list of the constellations is provided in the Appendix (see page 172).

So, let's wrap up warm, get outside, give our eyes a good 40 minutes to adjust to the darkness, and start to find our way around the stars of the spring sky.

Spring sky in the northern hemisphere

The charts represent how the sky will look at the following times:

- 16 February at 00:30
- 15 March at 22:30
- 15 April at 20:30

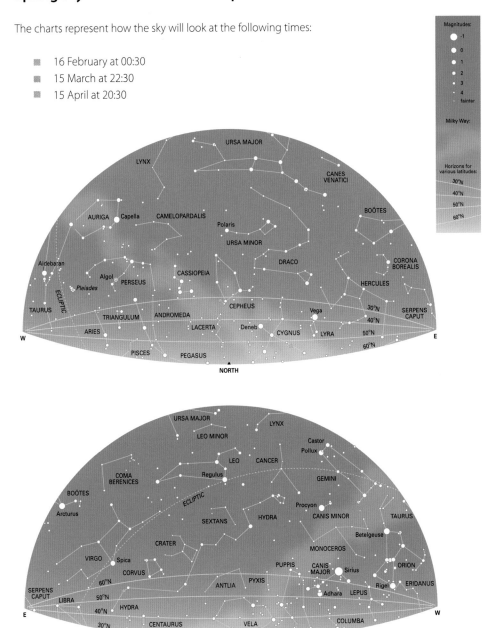

▲ *The spring sky is full of prominent and easy-to-spot constellations like Gemini and Leo to the south.*

We will start our journey around the spring sky in the south, which is dominated by the constellation Leo – unlike most of the constellations, this actually looks like the lion it is supposed to resemble. If you are not sure where south is then you can find it easily enough by thinking about the direction that the Sun sets, which is due west. From facing west, south is the direction that your left shoulder is pointing. Turning to face south, look in the sky about halfway between the horizon and overhead and you should be able to see a backwards question mark, which represents the head of the lion. At the base of the question mark is the star Regulus, a bright blue-white star with a magnitude of 1.4, making it the 21st brightest star in the sky. The rest of Leo's body can be seen stretching out to the east.

If you now turn around and face the opposite direction, you will be looking north – and nearly overhead is the constellation Ursa Major with the famous Plough (or Big Dipper) pattern of stars. It also looks like a giant saucepan being held upside down as though all its contents are being poured out. The Plough is an excellent place to start hopping around the sky and following the curve of the tail takes us to the beautiful orange star Arcturus, in Boötes. If we follow the curve on even further, it takes us to Spica, the brightest star in the rather fainter but larger constellation of Virgo.

While facing north you might spot a bright star twinkling away down near the horizon to the right. This is Vega, which is one of the circumpolar stars we mentioned in Chapter 1, and like the majority of the stars in Ursa Major, it never set from the UK. Now find the two stars which make up the top of the bowl in the Plough, which in the sky appears at the bottom because it is now upside-down. Follow them along to the west and you will see a yellow star called Capella, in the constellation Auriga, and continue along towards the west to the faint star cluster called the Pleiades and the constellation Taurus.

Starting back at the bowl of the Plough, the two end stars on the western side are called the 'pointers' – following them down to the northern horizon points towards the Pole Star, known as Polaris. This star barely moves – only a tiny amount of motion is detectable during long-exposure photographs. If you follow the pointer stars in the other direction to the south, you will come across the familiar sight of Leo again, with Capella over in the western sky. Between the two is the constellation Gemini, which is easily identifiable by the two bright stars Castor and Pollux. Between Gemini and Leo is the much fainter constellation Cancer and, if you look carefully, you might just be able to spot another star cluster called the Beehive Cluster. It is similar to the Pleiades Cluster over in the north-west, but quite a bit fainter so binoculars will help to locate it.

Spring constellation focus

Leo is prominent in the south during the spring months and can be easily recognized by the backwards question mark representing the lion's head. The blue-white star Regulus is easy to spot at the base of the question mark, or 'sickle' as it is often called. Through binoculars Regulus, or Alpha Leonis, can be seen to be joined by a pair of companions which shine at eighth magnitude and appear off to the north-west. The entire multiple star system lies about 77 light years away, so we are seeing Regulus and its companions as they were 77 years ago.

Just 7° to the north of Regulus and a little to the east is another binary star called Algieba, or Gamma Leonis. The two component stars form a beautiful pair in small telescopes, appearing as yellow and orange stars just a tiny fraction of a degree apart. The rest of the stars making up the head of Leo arc round to the west, and about 20° to the east is Zosma, which represents the lion's back. By about the same distance out to the south-east is the second brightest star in the constellation called Denebola, which marks the tail. Completing a triangle with Denebola and Zosma is Chertan, a third-magnitude star which appears white in colour.

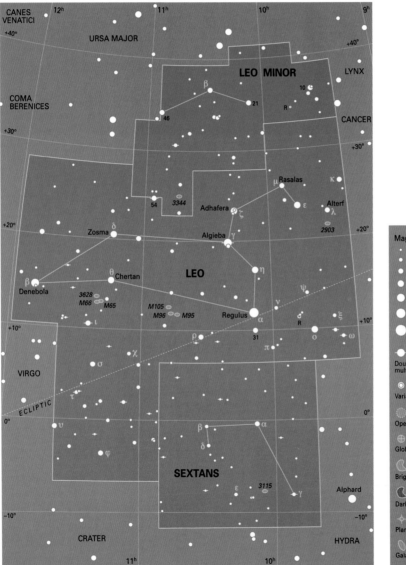

▲ *Leo is a great spring-time constellation that is home to some fine galaxies.*

Dropping a line down from Chertan will point us in the direction of the two stars that mark out Leo's hind legs, Iota Leonis which is the closest and Sigma Leonis which is about twice the distance. About halfway between Iota Leonis and Chertan lie a beautiful pair of galaxies named M65 and M66. These galaxies are amongst the recognized 110 objects in a catalogue that was compiled by Charles Messier in the 18th century. Both objects are spiral galaxies shining at ninth magnitude, which means a decent pair of binoculars should just be able to pick them out. They are definitely easy to spot in small telescopes but larger instruments will reveal that the pair are joined by a third companion, called NGC 3628, just over a degree to the north.

There is another cluster of galaxies a little under halfway between Chertan and Regulus, but they are a little fainter than M65 and M66 so a small telescope is needed to see them clearly. The members of this cluster are M95, M96 and M105. M95 is my favourite galaxy out of all of them as it appears as a beautiful barred spiral galaxy face-on to us, so we can see the structure of the spiral arms. Just to the east of M95 is the spiral galaxy M96, the most distant of the group at around 41 million light years, and to its north-east is M105, a giant elliptical galaxy with a diameter of around 35,000 light years.

Ursa Major, known as the Great Bear, is without doubt one of the most well known of all the constellations. From latitudes comparable with much of the UK it never sets and within its borders lies the easily identifiable asterism known as the Plough, the Saucepan or the Big Dipper. The stars of the Plough are the seven brightest stars in the constellation and they act as great pointers around the rest of the sky, as we saw in the spring sky guide on page 38.

Just 5° (remember you can estimate this as half of the width of your fist held at arm's length) to the north of Alkaid, the blue-white star at the easternmost tip of the handle of the Plough, lies a beautiful example of a face-on spiral galaxy, known as M101. It is about twice the size of the Milky Way, making it one of the largest spiral galaxies known, and although it lies relatively close to us at about 27 million light years it does require a larger telescope to see it in its full glory. Any telescope from about 10 cm or more will be able to detect the light from the billions of stars in its core, but a telescope with a larger aperture will be needed to detect the subtle details in its spiral arms.

The next star along in the handle of the Plough is Mizar which, with its companion Alcor, makes a stunning view in binoculars. The two stars were once used as a test of good eyesight before modern tests were developed because only people with good eyesight are able to see the two individually. The pair were once thought to be an optical binary star system, which

◀ *The beautiful spiral galaxies M81 (left) and M82, which can be found in Ursa Major.*

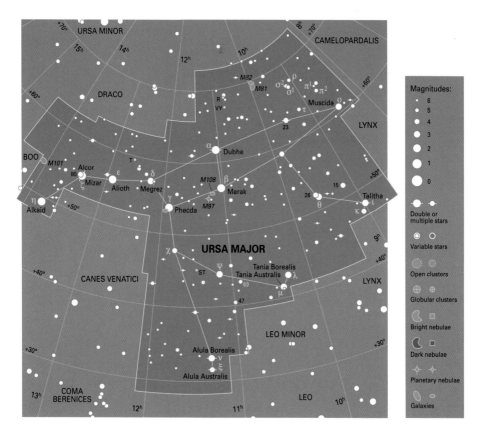

Magnitudes:
- 6
- 5
- 4
- 3
- 2
- 1
- 0

Double or multiple stars

Variable stars

Open clusters

Globular clusters

Bright nebulae

Dark nebulae

Planetary nebulae

Galaxies

▲ *Ursa Major is one of the easiest constellations to spot, with its famous Plough (Big Dipper) asterism.*

means they are not linked gravitationally, but careful studies have shown that the two are moving through space in the same direction, suggesting that they are indeed related. Mizar is the closest of the two at 78 light years while Alcor is 3 light years more distant, and by studying the hidden messages in their light, previously unseen companions have been revealed.

Alioth is the next star along the handle and the brightest star in Ursa Major. Moving west along the handle leads us to Megrez, the first star in the bowl of the dipper, or if we consider the Great Bear then it is the star which joins his tail to his hind. The bowl extends to the south taking in Phecda and, further to the west, the pointers Merak and Dubhe. A line between these two and extended up to the north leads to the north Pole Star, Polaris, which has been used by sailors for centuries to find north. About 3° to the east of Merak lies a beautiful example of a planetary nebula, known as the Owl Nebula (M97). It is unfortunately quite a faint object so smaller telescopes will only show it as a fuzzy blob – it requires a telescope of around 20 cm aperture to be able to see its owl-like features.

Another treat lies in store within the bounds of Ursa Major and it can be found by extending a line between Phecda and Dubhe out to the north-west for about the same distance again. Here you will find two beautiful galaxies called M81 and M82. M81 is without doubt one of the most rewarding spiral galaxies in the northern hemisphere for amateur observation, and at magnitude 6.9 it can just be seen in binoculars from a dark site. With the larger light grasp of a telescope it is possible to see more detail, and anything over about 20 cm aperture will easily reveal structure in the spiral arms. M82 lies just over half a degree to the north of M81 and low magnification will reveal them both in the same field of view. Unlike M82, M81 looks cigar-shaped even through small telescopes, but detailed observations have revealed that M81 was recently disturbed by M82, causing a burst in star formation. Both galaxies lie at a distance of about 12 million light years away so we see them as they appeared 12 million years ago!

The rest of the stars in Ursa Major extend to the west and south of the Plough, which itself represents the bear's tail and hind. Although it is a large constellation, these stars are not bright when compared to the Plough so dark skies are needed to pick them out.

Gemini is a nice easy constellation to pick out in the spring sky, as it appears like a large rectangle out to the west of Leo. The two brighter stars are found on the north-east edge of the rectangle, with the white star Castor to the top and the yellow star Pollux at the bottom. Although Castor appears as a single star to the naked eye, it is actually a complex multiple star system consisting of six stars in three pairs, all gravitationally linked. Pollux, on the other hand, is a single orange giant star and is the brightest in Gemini. To the south-west of Pollux by about 20° is the third brightest star in the constellation, called Alhena. It is also a spectroscopic binary star, which means its companion can only be detected through the careful study of its spectrum.

There are three stars that lie between Pollux and Alhena, all of which are around fourth magnitude so a dark site is needed to see them all. The central star of the three is called Delta

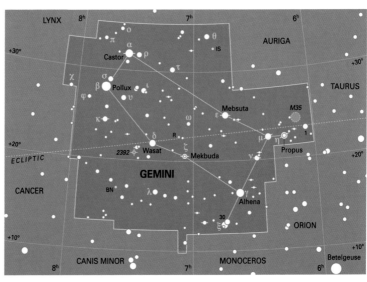

▲ *Gemini is an easy-to-spot, moderately bright constellation with its two brightest stars, Castor and Pollux, near its western border.*

▲ *Open clusters M35 and NGC 2158 can be found in Gemini.*

Geminorum and it lies just 2° to the north-west of the Eskimo Nebula (NGC 2392). This fine example of a planetary nebula lies around 4,000 light years away and, at magnitude 9.8, a good-sized telescope is needed to see it at its best. Telescopes larger than 15 cm start to reveal structure in the fuzzy circular blob, but those around 25 cm or more will clearly show a dark ring breaking up the disk, which makes the whole thing resemble the face of an eskimo surrounded by a big fluffy hood.

If you imagine a giant rectangle with three of its points at Castor, Pollux and Alhena, then the final point would be marked by Mu Geminorum. This is the fourth brightest star in Gemini and, along with other bright stars surrounding it, depicts the foot of one of the twins which the constellation represents. It looks noticeably red to the naked eye, telling us that it is a low-temperature star. Its visible surface temperature is estimated at around 3,600°C, and as it nears the end of its life it will cool further, until its outer layers are shed out into space. Estimates of its mass suggest it has three times as much material as the Sun, yet due to its stage of evolution it has swollen in size to about 100 times the solar radius.

Lying along the Milky Way, Gemini is rich in beautiful swathes of glittering stars, but there is one patch known as M35 which is deserving of attention and it can be found about 3° to the north-west of Mu Geminorum. It can just be detected with the naked eye from dark sites with good observing conditions, but looks amazing through small telescopes with low magnifications. There are about 150 stars in this cluster, but it is difficult to differentiate them from other stars in the Milky Way which provide a backdrop. It is relatively close to us at 2,800 light years and has a diameter of about 24 light years, which means light from a star on one edge would take 24 years to reach a star on the other edge of the cluster. This cluster should not be confused with NGC 2158, which is a much fainter and smaller cluster to the south-west, and although it is roughly the same actual size as M35, it is much further away at an estimated 16,500 light years.

Summer sky in the northern hemisphere

The charts represent how the sky will look at the following times:

- 16 May at 02:00
- 16 June at 00:00
- 15 July at 22:00

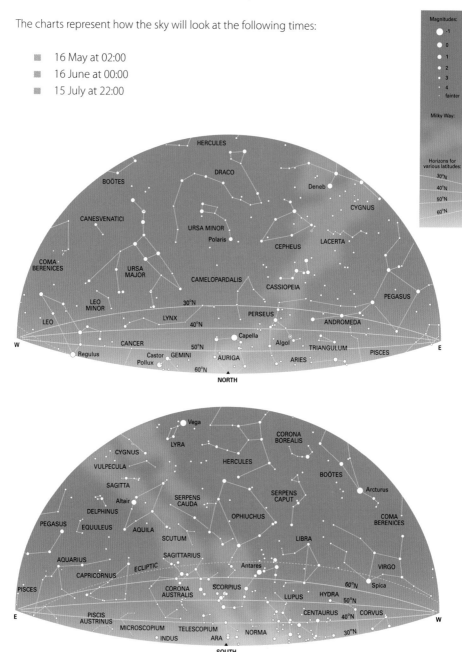

▲ *The summer sky is home to dozens of galaxies that are within easy reach of a beginner's telescope.*

One of the challenges with summertime astronomy is that you have to stay up quite late to get a dark sky, but from some extreme latitudes you never get a truly dark sky in the summer. You will notice the times for the summer charts are quite late, to allow us to get the most out of the treats lying in wait for us. We start our tour of the summer sky by facing to the west, which you will remember is the direction of the setting Sun. You will notice the familiar stars of Leo low in the west and, high above, the constellation Ursa Major as it continues its relentless journey around the celestial pole.

The stars in the Plough, which resemble the hind and tail of Ursa Major, are great pointers around the rest of the sky. If you draw a line between the stars Dubhe and Phecda, at the north-west and south-east corners of the bowl of the Plough, and extend the line down towards the horizon then eventually you will find a bright first-magnitude star called Spica, the brightest star in Virgo. The rest of the stars in the constellation are significantly fainter and extend northwards from Spica.

From the handle of the Plough, follow its curve on towards the southern horizon to find the bright star Arcturus, which sits at the southern end of the constellation Boötes. Arcturus is easy to spot as it is a bright red star only one magnitude fainter than Spica, which is to its south. Just to the east of Boötes is the constellation called Hercules and it can be easily located by looking for the 'keystone' group of stars that form a square shape. It is home to the stunning globular cluster known as M13, and we will look at this in more detail in the next section overleaf.

High in the south-east beyond Hercules are three bright stars which together form the Summer Triangle. This unofficial grouping of stars is easy to pick out in the darkening twilight sky and is depicted by Vega in Lyra, Deneb in Cygnus and Altair in Aquila. If you are unsure how to locate it then take the two stars on the eastern side of the bowl of the Plough (these

▲ *The beautiful Hercules Globular Cluster is also known as M13 or NGC 6205.*

are the two which make up the side opposite to the pointers) and continue their line out to the east until you find Deneb in Cygnus. This blue-white star marks out the north-east tip of the triangle, with Vega in Lyra marking the north-west tip and finally Altair in Aquila to the south. These bright stars are great for helping to identify the constellations within which they reside, but it is worth hunting down the star at the centre of the triangle, which is a beautiful binary star known as Albireo.

If you can imagine a curved line from Albireo to Altair in Aquila, then sweep through that line slowly to find the famous Coathanger Cluster, which is shaped like a giant inverted celestial coathanger. Binoculars are by far the best way to see this cluster, which is just over 4,000 light years away. Another little treat lies to the east of the Coathanger by about 10°, the Dumbbell Nebula, which is a stunning stellar corpse just visible in binoculars from dark skies. Low- to medium-power telescopes will show this object to have a markedly dumbbell shape. Both the Coathanger and the Dumbbell are found in a small and faint constellation known as Vulpecula, which sits between Cygnus and Sagitta, another small constellation which borders Aquila.

If you have a clear southern border and the sky is clear to the horizon, then you may be able to pick out a cluster of moderately bright stars. Resembling a trapezium, this group of four bright stars to the south-east are members of Sagittarius, which unfortunately never rises very high from moderate northern latitudes. To the west is Antares, a bright red star which is the brightest star in the constellation Scorpius, whose head can be seen poking up above the horizon.

Summer constellation focus

Hercules lies high in the south during summer months and darker skies are needed to see all of its mostly faint stars. To find it, locate the brightest star between Arcturus and Altair, known as Alpha Ophiuchus, and just to its west by a couple of degrees is the brightest star in Hercules, Alpha Herculis. It is also called Rasalgethi, which means 'head of the kneeler', giving a clue to the fact that the whole shape of Hercules is actually shown upside down in northern skies. Alpha Herculis is a variable red-giant star nearing the end of its life, a fate that awaits our Sun. It is joined by a companion star, which can be easily seen through telescopes, and due to the contrast between them both, they appear as a stunning red-and-green duet.

To the north of Alpha Herculis by about 5° is the famous 'keystone' shape of stars, which looks like a slightly misshapen square. Zeta Herculis is the brightest star of the group and sits at the south-west corner; to its east is Epsilon Herculis and moving around the square in a clockwise direction takes us to Pi Herculis, and finally on to Eta Herculis. Two-thirds of the way down between Eta and Zeta Herculis is the beautiful Hercules Globular Cluster, also known as M13. At magnitude 5.8, the cluster is visible as a hazy patch to the naked eye, but even a small telescope will easily start to reveal individual stars in the cluster. It is interesting to compare the view of the cluster through different sized telescopes, as increasing aperture will not only reveal a brighter image but also more stars as the resolving power of the telescope increases (see Chapter 3 for a description of resolving power). The cluster owes its prominence in our sky due to its relative proximity to us at a little over

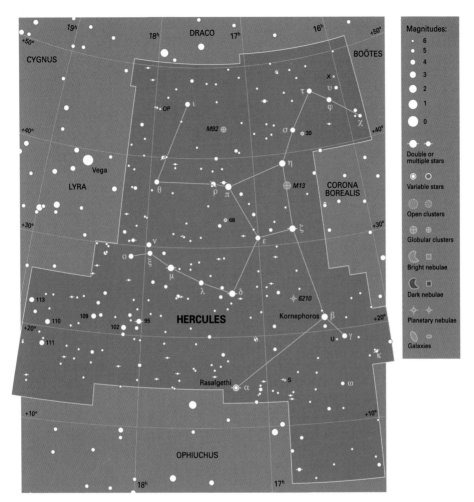

▲ *Hercules is a great summer constellation and is home to the great globular cluster M13.*

25,000 light years. It is thought that the cluster contains up to a million stars yet is only around 150 light years in diameter. If we lived on a planet in orbit around a star in the centre of the cluster, the sky would be full of thousands of stars brighter than the planet Venus.

Cygnus is the largest of the three constellations making up the Summer Triangle and its brightest star, Deneb, marks its north-eastern corner. It is thought that Deneb lies around 1,500 light years from us, although its exact distance is unknown. We can compare its brightness to its distance and, because brightness fades with increasing distance, it is possible to work out how bright it really is. The brightness we observe in the sky means in reality it is around 55,000 times brighter than the Sun. It marks the tail of Cygnus, the Swan, with his body and neck pointing over towards the south-west and the centre of the Summer Triangle.

Gamma Cygni is the next star in line along the body of Cygnus and is a rather unusual type of yellow supergiant star, because most are either red and cool or blue and hot, yet this ageing yellow supergiant has a moderate temperature! Next is Eta Cygni which is fainter than Gamma, but one of the real showcases of Cygnus is the next star, known as Albireo. It is easy to find as it sits centrally in the Summer Triangle and is an object well worth spending some time looking at. Even a small telescope will reveal the binary nature of this star as it separates under magnification into two stunning stars, yellow and blue in colour. The system is 380 light years away, but it is not yet known whether they are a true binary system in orbit around each other. If they are, then the orbital period is thought to be around 70,000 years. The yellow star in the Albireo pair is also a binary star system, with a fainter companion visible in only the largest of amateur telescopes with apertures of 50 cm or more.

The stars representing the wings of Cygnus stretch out from Gamma Cygni and are easily seen from moderately dark sites. The wing to the north-west is marked by second-magnitude Delta Cygni, which is a triple star system resolvable in moderate-sized telescopes, while the south-eastern wing is marked by Epsilon Cygni, which is marginally brighter than Delta.

Cygnus is home to a couple of open clusters, but they are hidden somewhat by the rich swathes of stars of the Milky Way behind. M29 is the first and faintest of the two but is quite an easy object to spot in binoculars, just a couple of degrees to the east of Gamma Cygni. Through a telescope the cluster looks nice and has a box-like shape to it from the 30 or so member stars. M39 is the other cluster, which can just be seen with the naked eye from a

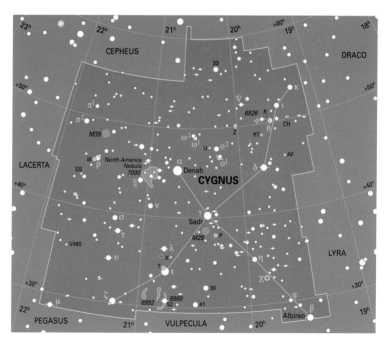

▲ *Deneb in Cygnus is one of the three stars making up the Summer Triangle asterism, the others being Vega (in Lyra) and Altair (in Aquila).*

▲ *The North America Nebula (NGC 7000) in Cygnus is a good target for wide-field telescopes but requires a dark sky to spot.*

dark site and can be found by drawing a line between Albireo and Gamma Cygni and then imagining extending it out to the north-east for roughly the same distance again. It covers an area of sky just over half a degree, making it larger in appearance than the full Moon. Binoculars are by far the best instrument to use to observe this cluster because of its large size, which is mainly due to its relatively close proximity at around 800 light years.

There are some wonderful examples of nebulae in Cygnus and the North America Nebula is probably the easiest to spot. It can be found just a couple of degrees to the north-east of Deneb and can be seen with the unaided eye from a dark site. It will only appear as a diffuse glow, almost like a detached part of the Milky Way, but turning binoculars or a telescope with a low-power, wide-field eyepiece on the area will reveal its nebulous nature. The entire nebula stretches far across the sky, covering an area 3° × 2.5°, and resembles the shape of the North American continent. For telescope owners trying to spot the nebula, keep to low magnifications but try using a narrowband filter like the O III (pronounced 'Oh-three') and you will be amazed how it pops into view.

The Veil Nebula is another object worth hunting down – like the North America Nebula it requires dark skies, wide-field telescopes and narrowband filters to really enhance the view. The nebula is the remains of a star that exploded over 5,000 years ago and can be seen with great loops of wispy nebulosity. The eastern segment is the brightest portion of the nebula and requires excellent observing conditions to be able to detect it with the naked eye.

Lyra lies to the west of Cygnus and is home to Vega, the fifth brightest star in the sky and the north-west corner of the Summer Triangle. The constellation is small compared to Cygnus and is composed primarily of Vega and a small parallelogram of stars just to its south-east.

Magnitudes:
- 6   • 2
- 5   • 1
- 4   • 0
- 3

Double or multiple stars

Variable stars

Open clusters

Globular clusters

Bright nebulae

Dark nebulae

Planetary nebulae

Galaxies

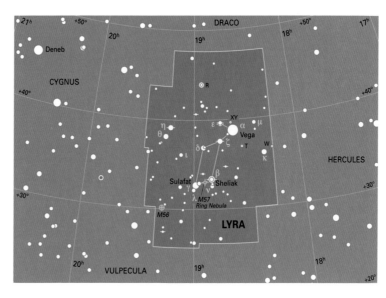

▲ *Lyra is a small constellation in the summer sky which is home to the Ring Nebula.*

Zeta Lyrae lies just under 5° to Vega's south-east and marks the north-western corner of the parallelogram, which is a fascinating multiple star system. To the naked eye it looks like a fairly average fourth-magnitude star, but even a small telescope splits it into two, although high magnification from larger telescopes reveals that there are actually seven component stars. Forming a triangle with Vega and Zeta Lyrae is a well-known multiple star system called Epsilon Lyrae, which is affectionately known as 'the Double Double'. Binoculars will reveal that the star is actually two individual components of roughly the same brightness, but good-quality telescopes of 15 cm or more should be able to separate the stars further. The northern pair of stars are separated by just 2.8 arc seconds, whereas the southern pair are separated by slightly less, at 2.6 arc seconds. There are a total of five stars in this system, as the brighter star in the northern pair is a spectroscopic binary, which means the presence of the other star is only visible by a detailed inspection of the spectrum of the star.

Delta Lyrae marks the north-eastern corner of the parallelogram and although it appears to be a naked-eye binary star, the two components are not gravitationally linked and are thought to be separated by at least 3 light years. They are still a nice sight in binoculars or a small telescope. The southern edge of the parallelogram is found just under 5° to the south and is marked by Gamma Lyrae to the east and Beta Lyrae to the west. One of the real treasures of the summer sky is found directly between these two stars – it can be glimpsed through binoculars from a dark site but a telescope reveals its true splendour. Turning your telescope on this location will reveal the ghostly circular glow that is M57, or the Ring Nebula. Dark skies and suitable magnification will show a darker central region to the disk, giving a clue to its nature as a planetary nebula. M57 is probably the best example of this type of object, which is an expanding spherical shell of gas, the aftermath of a star that died millions of years ago.

Autumn sky in the northern hemisphere

The charts represent how the sky will look at the following times:

- 16 August at 00:30
- 15 September at 22:30
- 15 October at 20:30

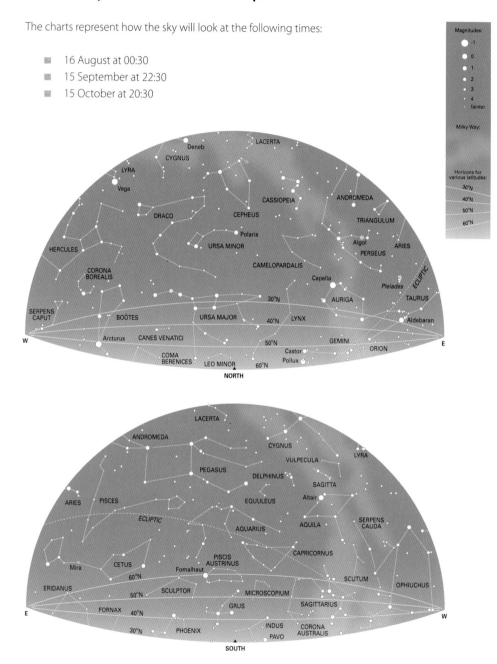

▲ *As the sky darkens in autumn, it is a great opportunity to study our own Galaxy, the Milky Way.*

High in the south-west is the magnificent view of the Summer Triangle with the familiar stars of Vega, Deneb and Altair. The Plough and Ursa Major are now low in the north-west, with the autumn constellations dominating the sky. Pointing down from the Pole Star, Polaris, towards the north-west horizon is a smaller version of the Plough called Ursa Minor. It represents a small bear, and skirting between it and Ursa Major is the large rambling constellation called Draco, the Dragon. There are no bright stars in Draco so dark skies and good clear weather are needed to pick it out. On the opposite side of the Pole Star from Ursa Major is the easy-to-recognize shape of Cassiopeia, the Queen. It actually looks nothing like the queen on her throne but instead is easy to spot as a giant celestial 'W' on its side. Cassiopeia is a great pointer to a couple of other autumn constellations, Perseus and Cepheus. On the southern side of Cassiopeia is a noticeably yellow star, Alpha Cassiopeiae, and a line from here to the west to Beta Cassiopeiae points to Cepheus. Cepheus looks like a child's drawing of a house with the roof pointing over to the north-east.

Heading back through the 'W' of Cassiopeia from Alpha Cassiopeiae leads us on first to Gamma and then Delta Cassiopeiae, and a line joining the two and extended onwards points towards Perseus over in the east. Perseus is easy to spot as it has a bright curve of stars open towards the pole. Following the curve of Perseus on towards the east leads to the bright yellow light of Capella in Auriga. Joining up Gamma and Alpha Cassiopeiae and extending the line down towards the southern horizon points to the Great Square of Pegasus and Andromeda.

The Square of Pegasus is a true sign that autumn is here and it dominates the southern sky at this time of year. Pegasus was the winged horse in mythology and its great Square covers an area of sky around 15° × 15°, marked out by four second-magnitude stars. The rest of Pegasus stretches out to the west towards Aquila and the Summer Triangle. Alpheratz is the star at the north-east corner of the Square, but it is also a member of the neighbouring constellation Andromeda, which stretches away from the Square off to the north-east and is home to the famous Andromeda Galaxy, which is just visible to the naked eye.

Joining a line between Scheat in the north-west corner of the Square of Pegasus and Alpheratz in the north-east and extending it towards the east points towards the tiny constellation beyond Andromeda called Triangulum. From dark sites it might just be possible to see the giant galaxy known as M33, or the Pinwheel Galaxy. At a distance of 2.8 million light years, it is amongst the most distant objects that can be glimpsed with the naked eye. It is easiest if you scan the sky about 4° to the west of Alpha Trianguli, which is the second brightest star in the constellation. Moving on further in the same direction leads to Aries and its brightest star, Hamal.

Taking a different line from Scheat through Algenib to the south-east and extending towards the south-eastern horizon takes you first through Pisces and then on through to the constellation Cetus, the Whale. Both of these constellations are quite faint and because they are relatively low down near the horizon they can be tricky to spot if the weather conditions are not great. Moving westwards back towards Altair again, we find the stars of Aquarius low in the south and Capricornus just to its south-west.

Autumn constellation focus

Perseus is edging round to the south-east in the autumn sky and has a prominent curve of reasonably bright stars, which makes it relatively easy to identify just to the east of Cassiopeia. Mirfak is the brightest of its stars and is located by drawing a line from Gamma and Delta Cassiopeiae to the east. It is 590 light years away and shines at a magnitude of 1.82, which tells us that it is kicking out as much energy as around 5,000 Suns. It is only just brighter than Beta Persei, otherwise known as Algol, which is just 10° to its south and is without doubt the most famous star in the constellation.

Algol is a multiple star system, with three stars all in orbit around each other. Two of the stars, Beta Persei A and Beta Persei B, orbit along our line of sight, so although normally we see the combined magnitude of 2.1, every 2 days 20 hours and 49 minutes its brightness dips to 3.4 when the fainter star eclipses the brighter star. There is another dip in brightness when the brighter star eclipses the fainter, but this is only detectable through the careful study of the system's spectrum. Algol was the first eclipsing binary system discovered like this so others like it are classed as *Algol variables*.

To the south-east of Algol by about 10° is a line of three stars: Epsilon Persei to the north, Xi Persei in the centre and Zeta Persei to the south. Just half a degree to the north of Xi Persei is a large faint region of nebulosity known as the California Nebula. It shines at fourth magnitude, but because that light is spread over a large area it has low surface brightness, making it challenging to see visually. Wide-field telescopes, dark skies and crystal clear

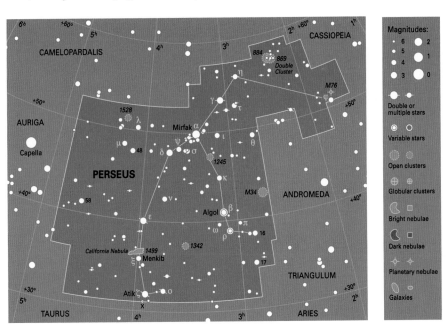

▲ *Perseus is an inconspicuous constellation but it's worth hunting down for the Double Cluster, which lies in the direction of Cassiopeia.*

▲ *The Double Cluster (NGC 869 and NGC 884), as seen in the constellation of Perseus.*

skies are essential to pick it up, but your chances can be increased with the use of an H-beta filter. The nebula is a vast cloud of hydrogen gas and dust about 1,000 light years away and around 100 light years across, out of which new stars are being born.

Moving north-west from Mirfak in the direction of Cassiopeia leads to Gamma Persei, which is the fifth brightest star in Perseus, shining at magnitude 2.9. About 4° further along is Eta Persei, a stunning binary star 1,300 light years away. Through even a modest telescope the two component stars appear gold and blue, making them very similar in appearance to Albireo in Cygnus. About 5° to the west of Eta Persei and close to the stars of Cassiopeia lie NGC 869 and NGC 884, a beautiful pair of star clusters just visible to the naked eye as a faint hazy patch of light. The two clusters are collectively known as the Perseus Double Cluster and each measures about half a degree in diameter, which is about the same as the diameter of the full Moon. Due to their large apparent size in the sky, they are best observed using either binoculars or a telescope with low power to give a nice wide field of view. Compared to most clusters, they are young with an estimated age of around 12 million years, which we can tell by the population of young hot blue-white stars.

Pegasus is one of the most noticeable constellations in the autumn sky, with the easily recognized great Square of Pegasus dominant. In the northern hemisphere sky it appears as the upside-down front half of the winged horse, with the Square representing the main body, the head extending down to the south-west and the front legs to the north-west. The brightest star in the Square is found to the north-east and is known as Alpheratz, which also forms part of the constellation of Andromeda to the north-east. To its west is Scheat, the second brightest star in the Square and noticeably orange in colour. Round to the south is Markab and completing the Square is Algenib to the south-east.

Just to the west of Scheat and Markab are two fainter stars: Mu Pegasi and Lambda Pegasi (Lambda Pegasi is a little fainter and further away than Mu Pegasi). Almost halfway between Mu Pegasi and Markab is a faint fifth-magnitude star called 51 Pegasi. It can just be seen with the naked eye from a dark site and telescopically it does not look much, but it was the first sunlike star to have a planet discovered in orbit around it.

About 7° to the north of Mu Pegasi is Eta Pegasi, which is a little fainter than Scheat to its east. Drawing a line between Mu and Eta Pegasi and extending it out to the north for around the same distance leads to NGC 7331, a lovely example of a spiral galaxy. From our vantage point it is seen almost edge-on, and the presence of prominent dust lanes among the spiral arms means there is quite a lot of detail to be seen visually. At magnitude 9, it is easily visible in small telescopes and from a dark site the dust lanes can even be glimpsed. Pictures of this beautiful galaxy nearly 50 million light years away can reveal the galaxy in all its glory, but telescopes with equatorial mounts and drives are needed to capture it.

Taking a line from Algenib at the south-east corner of the Square through Markab at the south-west corner and out for the same distance again to the west points to the location of the globular cluster M15. If it were not for M13, the great cluster in Hercules, then M15 would be given more attention, but it is sadly overlooked. Binoculars or a small telescope will reveal it as a fuzzy-looking star, but telescopes of 15 cm aperture or more will start to show the individual stars making up this cluster. It is about 35,000 light years away and measures around 200 light years in diameter, with over 100,000 member stars.

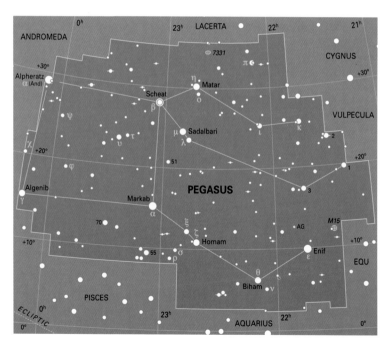

▲ *Pegasus is easy to find and its great 'Square' can help direct you to other constellations.*

Globular clusters like M15 contain high quantities of older stars, unlike open clusters which contain mostly younger stars, and in the case of M15 it is thought to be one of the oldest clusters at an estimated 12 billion years.

Andromeda is found to the north-east corner of Pegasus and indeed Alpha Andromedae is the star depicting the north-east corner of the Square of Pegasus. Heading to the north-east from Alpha Andromedae, or Alpheratz as it is commonly known, is a line of stars and the first we come across is third-magnitude Delta Andromedae. The next one along is Mirach, which shines at the same brightness as Alpheratz but is a cool red giant in contrast to the blue-white of Alpheratz. It is about 200 light years away and is so large that if it were in the position of the Sun it would almost swallow up the orbit of Mercury.

Moving further east is Almach, a stunning second-magnitude multiple star system within easy reach of small telescopes. Even the smallest will reveal two of the stars, one appearing golden-yellow in colour and the other blue, although some observers report it as appearing green! The fainter blue/green star is also a double star, but the two are separated by just 0.5 arc second so a telescope of at least 30 cm aperture is needed to split them. The brighter of these two is also double, making this a complex four-star system, although this last one is only detectable through the careful study of the spectrum of the system.

About 4° to the east of Almach is a lovely edge-on spiral galaxy called NGC 891, which, through even small telescopes, is revealed as a needle-thin smudge of light. Anything from

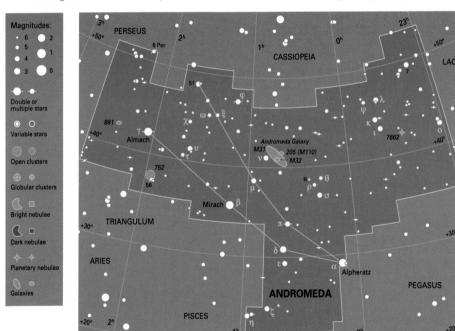

▲ *Andromeda is home to the Andromeda Galaxy, which is easy to see from a dark site even with the naked eye.*

▲ *This image shows NGC 891, an edge-on spiral galaxy in the constellation of Andromeda.*

15 cm aperture and above will start to reveal detail in this galaxy 30 million light years away. A dark dust lane is visible along its equator in larger telescopes, dissecting the galaxy in two. It is now believed that this galaxy may actually have a bar, which cannot be seen in visible light due to its orientation, but piercing through the dust clouds the Hubble Space Telescope has detected concentrations of stars in a bar-like formation.

North-west from Mirach is Mu Andromedae, a faint star shining at magnitude 3.9, and a little further along is Nu Andromedae, even fainter at magnitude 4.5. If you scan the sky about 5° to the north-west of Nu Andromedae, you will see the Andromeda Galaxy as a faint fuzzy patch with the naked eye. The light that your eyes are detecting left the galaxy just over 2 million years ago, so you are seeing the galaxy as it was over 2 million years in the past. Binoculars will reveal a larger fuzzy patch of light, but point a telescope at the galaxy and anything from 20 cm and above should be able to start picking out detail in the spiral arms from a dark site. Telescopes of 15 cm aperture or more are able to detect the two satellite galaxies – M32 on the south-eastern side and M110 to the north-west. Unlike most galaxies in the Universe, the Andromeda Galaxy is moving towards us, at a rate of about 111 km/sec, which means its light is blue-shifted.

There are four fourth-magnitude stars lying to the west of the Andromeda Galaxy by about 12°. Just between the two most southerly stars, Iota and Omicron Andromedae, and a little further to the south is a beautiful planetary nebula called the Blue Snowball Nebula (NGC 7662). With a magnitude of 8.3, it is visible in small telescopes and anything above 15 cm will reveal a noticeably blue smudge of light. Larger instruments will reveal a slight darkening towards the centre.

Red shift and blue shift

Red shift is a well-known phenomenon where the movement of an object *away* from the observer causes its light to be shifted to the red end of the spectrum. Blue shift is the result of movement *towards* the observer, which causes light to move to the blue end of the spectrum.

Winter sky in the northern hemisphere

The charts represent how the sky will look at the following times:

- 16 November at 00:00
- 15 December at 22:00
- 15 January at 20:00

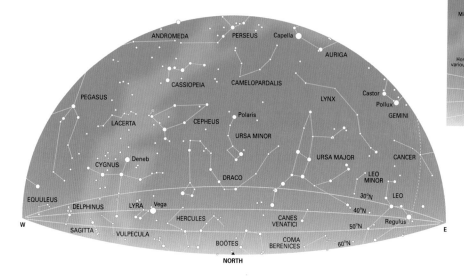

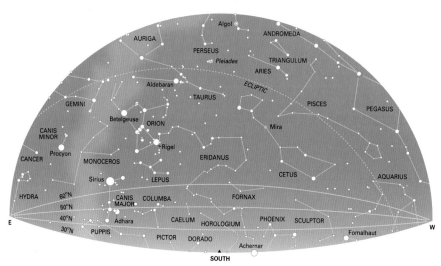

▲ *The long dark nights of winter mean conditions can be perfect for hunting down deep-sky wonders.*

The familiar summer constellations are long gone, with the stars of the Summer Triangle struggling to maintain prominence low in the north-west, while the autumn stars in Pegasus and Andromeda are sinking in the west. In the east are the stars which herald the approach of spring, but in the south the glittering stars of winter are now nicely positioned – and holding prime position in the south-east is Orion, the Hunter. Orion is easy to spot by looking for its famous three-star belt, which runs from south-east to north-west and is made up of three bright first-magnitude stars. The hunter's shoulders are depicted by the red giant Betelgeuse and the blue giant Bellatrix, with his feet marked by the white supergiant Rigel and the blue-coloured Saiph. The stars of Orion serve as great markers to the rest of the winter sky.

Following the belt stars down to the south-east leads to Sirius, the brightest star in the sky, which is in the constellation Canis Major. Sirius never rises much more than 20° above the horizon for UK observers and can often be seen twinkling away near the horizon. To the north-east of Sirius is the yellow star Procyon, which shines at magnitude 0.3 in the small constellation Canis Minor. To the west of Sirius and below Orion is a collection of fainter stars making up the constellation Lepus, the Hare. Extending a line from Orion's belt stars up to the north-west points towards the constellation Taurus, the Bull, which is recognizable by the 'V' shape of the Hyades star cluster marking the bull's head. Aldebaran is another bright red star like Betelgeuse and marks the eye of the bull on the cluster's southern side. A little further beyond Taurus is the Pleiades, which with a good pair of eyes and great observing conditions can be seen as a star cluster.

Extending a line along from the northern arm of the Hyades points towards Auriga with its brightest star, a yellow giant called Capella. To the west of Auriga is Perseus, which we looked at in the autumn sky section (see page 53), now sitting high in the south. The apex of the Hyades cluster points to the south-west and the fainter constellation of Cetus, the Whale, and between it and the lower half of Orion is Eridanus, the River. This is the largest constellation in the sky and weaves from the feet of Orion, passes Cetus, and wanders south near Fornax and deep into the southern-hemisphere sky, ending at around −60° declination. Gemini and Leo can be seen over in the east, and further round to the north the Plough can be seen standing on its end as it slowly rises into prominence in the coming spring months.

Winter constellation focus

Orion is without doubt one of the most fascinating constellations in the winter sky. It straddles the celestial equator with its famous three-star belt sitting partly in the northern hemisphere of the sky and partly in the southern hemisphere. The stars of the belt are all broadly the same brightness, although the central star, Alnilam, is over twice as far away as the other two stars, Alnitak to the south-east and Mintaka to the north-west. All three of the stars are roughly the same type and shine with a blue-white light that can be easily seen in the sky with the naked eye.

The entire constellation is bathed in nebulosity, but one of the more famous yet more elusive regions is the Horsehead Nebula, which can be seen just to the south of Alnitak. This is a dark nebula in the shape of a horsehead which is only visible because it is silhouetted against IC 434, a bright-red emission nebula sitting behind. Visually, it is very difficult to detect, requiring large-aperture telescopes and excellent transparent skies. Low-power eyepieces and an H-beta filter will help, but it is revealed much better in astronomical images of the area. To the east of Alnitak is another nebula known as the Flame Nebula, but this is a little easier to detect than the Horsehead. It lies at a distance of around 900 light years and covers an area of sky roughly the same size as the full Moon.

To the north of Alnitak by about 10° is one of Orion's most famous stars, Betelgeuse, whose name translates to 'armpit of the giant'. It is the second brightest star in Orion and shines with a distinctly red colour, which tells us that it is a relatively cool star with a surface temperature of around 3,100°C. Betelgeuse is a star nearing the end of its life that has used up all the hydrogen in its core and is now fusing helium into carbon and oxygen. Unlike our Sun, which has lived for just under 5 billion years, Betelgeuse is a supermassive star, which means it has rattled through its life much faster and is estimated to be only 6 million years old and already heading towards the end of its life.

The other shoulder is marked by Bellatrix, which is a first-magnitude blue-white binary star, and Orion's head is represented by Lambda Orionis. Underneath the belt stars are the feet of the hunter, with the blue-white supergiant Saiph marking his left foot and the other by Rigel, the brightest star in the constellation. Rigel has the Bayer designation of Beta Orionis but it is generally brighter than Alpha Orionis, otherwise known as Betelgeuse. This is due to the variable nature of Betelgeuse's brightness, which changes over a period of around

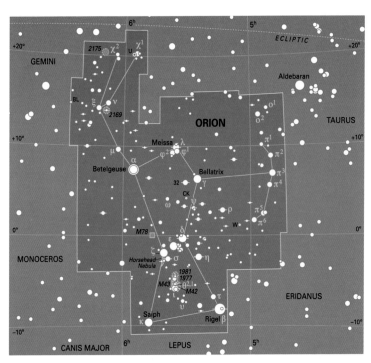

▲ *Orion is home to some stunning examples of nebulae, such as M42, which is my favourite object in Orion.*

▲ *A cluster of hot young stars in M42, the Orion Nebula.*

5.7 years due to the gentle pulsating of the size of the star. The white colour of Rigel's light tells us that it is hotter than our Sun with a surface temperature of around 11,000°C, which is almost double that of the Sun.

Turning our attention back to the belt stars again serves as a useful pointer to my favourite part of Orion, the Great Orion Nebula, which has a catalogue designation of M42. Find Alnilam, which you will recall is the middle star in the belt, and look for a faint line of three stars just below it. Look closely at the central 'star' and you will notice it looks rather fuzzy, which is very real and the result of the central star actually being a vast cloud of hydrogen gas and dust. Binoculars will show it a little more clearly but low-power telescopes reveal it in its full glory, with wispy filaments that arch around a central group of stars known as the Trapezium Cluster. The whole thing measures about 20 light years across and lies at a distance from us of around 1,300 light years, and is a stellar nursery where it is now thought nearly 700 new stars have formed. Visually, it looks grey-green in colour with the Trapezium Cluster clearly visible, but astronomical images reveal beautiful shades of red.

Taurus, the Bull, can be found by extending a line from the three belt stars of Orion up to the north-west to find a 'V' shape of stars. These are the stars of the Hyades Cluster, marking the head of Taurus – the piercing red colour of a star called Aldebaran marks the eye of the bull. The cluster is home to around 400 stars, but only five of them are visible to the naked eye, with more becoming visible in binoculars and small telescopes. Since its formation 625 million years ago, it will have lost a number of stars to the depths of interstellar space, and as the cluster ages further, more stars will drift away.

Aldebaran is not a member of the Hyades Cluster but lies about 80 light years closer, at a distance of 65 light years. It is a binary star system composed of an orange giant and a red dwarf star, both in orbit around each other, and there is also the possibility of a giant gas planet in orbit around the brighter star, but this is yet to be confirmed. Moving from Aldebaran to the north-east leads to Zeta Tauri, a blue giant with a surface temperature of around 22,000°C. Unlike most stars, its rotational speed at the equator is a staggering

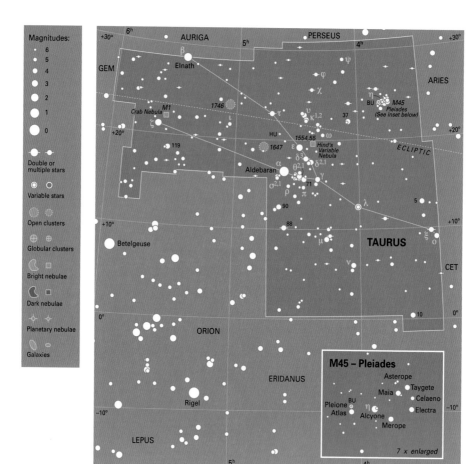

▲ *Two open clusters can be found in Taurus: the Hyades and the Pleiades.*

330 km/sec, which, although this is not fast enough to break the star up, does seem to relate in some way to a disk of material surrounding the star.

About 1° to the north-west of Zeta Tauri is the Crab Nebula, the remnant of a star which went supernova in 1054. It can just be detected as a fuzzy patch of light in binoculars, but telescopes of 15 cm aperture or more reveal its shape a little clearer. All massive stars suffer a violent death as the outer layers of the star get explosively ejected out into space as a supernova, leaving behind the dense core of the star. In the case of the Crab Nebula, which is M1 on Charles Messier's list, the core of the dead star is spinning at a rate of 30.2 times per second! This type of stellar corpse is known as a *pulsar*, based on the regular pulses of radiation detected here on Earth as it rotates.

Another cluster can be found in Taurus, lying 10° to the north-west of the Hyades. Visually, it looks much more like a cluster than the Hyades and is known as the Pleiades, or Seven Sisters. It gets its name from the seven stars visible to the naked eye, although great observing conditions and good eyesight are needed to see all of them. However, through binoculars and small telescopes with low-power eyepieces almost 100 stars become visible, although it is now believed the young cluster is home to around 500 stars. Long-exposure images of the cluster or observations through wide-field telescopes reveal faint blue nebulosity surrounding it, but spectroscopic studies reveal that the two are completely unrelated.

The rest of the constellation depicts the front legs of Taurus out to the south-west of the Hyades Cluster, as though the giant celestial bull is charging at Orion, who is depicted raising a shield and club at the bull. From the Hyades, one final part of the constellation runs from the northern part of the 'V' up to the north-east, towards the constellation Auriga, and it represents the bull's left horn. It ends in the first-magnitude star Elnath, which is the second brightest star in the constellation and is shared with the neighbouring constellation Auriga.

Auriga sits high in the winter sky and appears like a giant pentagon in the sky. Its southern-most star, Elnath, is shared with Taurus, while to the north of the constellation Capella shines as its brightest star. From UK latitudes, Capella never sets, making it a circumpolar star. It can be seen to have a distinctly yellow colour, which means its temperature is comparable to that of our Sun, although it is a little cooler. Amateur telescopes are unable to split it, but it is actually a binary star system composed of two stars similar to our Sun. Both are yellow, but both are about ten times the size of the Sun and 50 to 80 times more luminous.

To the south-west of Capella by about 5° is a triangle of third-magnitude stars known as the 'Kids'. The closest of the three to Capella is Epsilon Aurigae, which is a rather peculiar eclipsing binary star. Most eclipsing binary stars change in brightness by a magnitude or two every few days – however, in the case of Epsilon Aurigae, it drops by the same

▲ *The Pinwheel Cluster (M36) and the Starfish Cluster (M38) in the constellation of Auriga.*

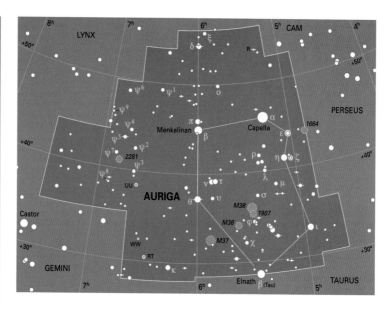

▲ *Auriga is home to three great binocular clusters: M36, M37 and M38.*

brightness but this happens every 27 years and lasts for two years! The cause of this is as yet unconfirmed, but it is likely that it is a companion star surrounded by a large unseen accretion disk.

Auriga is home to three lovely examples of open clusters, which can all be seen with binoculars and some with the naked eye. The first lies outside the pentagon shape to the east, roughly halfway between Elnath and Theta Aurigae. It is known as M37 and is the brightest cluster in the constellation. Binoculars reveal a sprinkling of stars but small telescopes reveal up to 150 members, most of which are blue-white but it also has nearly 20 red giant stars within its boundaries. This is without doubt one of the nicest telescopic open clusters to look at so is well worth hunting down.

To the west of M37 is M36, which is otherwise known as the Pinwheel Cluster. Telescopically, it is much less impressive than M37 as it has a lot fewer stars and none of them are red giants. A little further to the north-west is M38, the faintest of the three clusters in Auriga. With only 100 stars, M38 is not as impressive as M37, but, like the others, binoculars will reveal it as a mottled patch of light, while telescopes will resolve the majority of the cluster's stars.

Just a degree to the west of M36, the central of the three clusters, is a lovely combination of a stellar cluster and a region of nebulosity that is well worth seeking out. It tends to be referred to as NGC 1931, although that is the designation of the nebulosity rather than the cluster of stars. The whole thing measures just a few arc minutes across so it is a fraction the size of the full Moon, but it makes for a very pretty sight even though it is 10,000 light years away. The nebulosity represents the gas cloud that the cluster formed out of, but it is now being illuminated by the hot young stars it has just created.

MARK'S TOP TEN ASTRONOMICAL TARGETS

1. The crater Tycho on the Moon

This beautiful crater can be seen with the naked eye and measures 86 km across. It is surrounded by a system of rays, which are the result of the ejecta catapulted out of the

crater when it formed an estimated 108 million years ago. Analysis of the rock recovered by the Apollo 17 mission suggests the impactor may have been related to the same object that struck the Earth and ended the era of the dinosaurs. It is personal preference, but I think this feature looks best through binoculars or low-power telescopic magnification.

◀ *Tycho has a stunning ray system surrounding it.*

2. The rings of Saturn

Few people can fail to be impressed by the sight of the rings of the planet Saturn – indeed, they were the first things I saw through a telescope. The rings are made up of billions of pieces of ice and rock, spanning almost a quarter of a million kilometres at just under a kilometre thick. Their delicate structure is kept in place by orbiting moons and other gravitational effects. Due to the thin nature of the rings and the 'wobble' of Saturn on its axis, much like a child's spinning top, the rings are presented edge-on to us once every 15 years or so, and when this happens they disappear from view. Magnifications of at least 20× are needed to detect the rings.

▶ *Saturn wobbles on its axis just like a slow spinning top.*

3. The moons of Jupiter

Just as telescopes will reveal rings around Saturn, so they will also reveal moons around the largest planet in our Solar System, Jupiter. Even the low magnification from birdwatching telescopes will show the four Galilean satellites as they orbit around the planet. Keep watch over the period of a few hours and you will see that the moons slowly change their position. Sometimes it is possible to watch them disappear from view behind the planet, or even watch them move in front of the planet, and it is great to try and detect their tiny shadows as they do so. Higher magnifications of at least 100× and telescopes of at least 90 mm are needed to see these shadow transits.

▲ *Jupiter and its moons are a great target for observers with small telescopes.*

4. The polar caps on Mars

There are lots of features to see on Mars, but among the easiest to spot are the polar caps. Just like Earth, Mars has ice caps around the polar regions, but they are not made of water ice like ours; instead they are made of carbon dioxide ice. If you watch Mars over a period of months, you will see how the caps seem to shrink and grow as the planet experiences seasons just like ours. Telescopes are needed to see the polar caps and red filters can be used to enhance them.

◀ *Mars has loads to offer the visual observer, such as polar caps and dark rocky outcrops.*

5.   Albireo

Binary stars can be fairly uninspiring to look at, but there are a handful that are simply stunning. Albireo falls into the latter category, and even through powerful binoculars the yellow and blue component stars can be seen. It is found at the head of Cygnus, the Swan, in the centre of the unofficial asterism of stars known as the Summer Triangle. Telescopic observation is by far the best way to observe this and medium power is all that is required to split the two stars, which are separated by 615 thousand million kilometres.

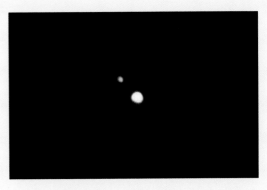

▲ *Albireo in Cygnus is a beautiful binary star system.*

6.   The Pleiades star cluster

This is one of the easiest deep-sky objects to detect with the naked eye and is found in the constellation Taurus. It gets its alternative name of the Seven Sisters from the seven brightest stars in the cluster, which have been used over the years as a test of good eyesight. In reality there are over 500 hot young stars in the Pleiades.

Low magnification is the best way to appreciate the beauty of this 100-million-year-old cluster, but long-exposure photographs will reveal the nebulosity that currently surrounds it. Studies of both show they are heading in different directions, though, so they are not related.

▶ *The nebulosity surrounding the Pleiades cluster is generally only visible in long-exposure photographs.*

7. The Ring Nebula

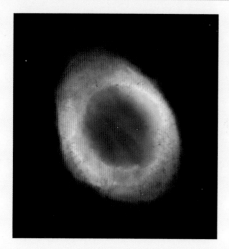

Not far from Albireo, in the neighbouring constellation of Lyra, is the Ring Nebula, which also goes by the catalogue number M57. It is a great example of a planetary nebula, which results at the death of stars with a similar mass to the Sun. It is supposedly visible in binoculars though I have never detected it, but point a telescope between the two stars at the base of the parallelogram in Lyra and there it is. It lies at just over 2,000 light years away and appears as a slightly elliptical smoke ring, and through much larger telescopes a central star is visible, which is the remains of the core of the star.

◀ *The Ring Nebula is a sphere of gas surrounding the core of a dead star.*

8. The Orion Nebula

Definitely worth hunting down as this is one of the easiest regions of nebulosity to detect visually and without any optical aid. We covered this in some detail earlier in this chapter and, as you will recall, it is visible in the winter sky just below the belt of Orion. It looks great even in binoculars and a telescope shows it off beautifully, but it can be enhanced with narrowband filters that are discussed in Chapter 5, such as the UHC, H-alpha or O III variety. Look closely at the object and you can see the Trapezium cluster of stars, which are just now starting to shine. This is a stellar nursery where stars are being born.

▶ *The Orion Nebula is found just to the south of Orion's three-star belt.*

9.   The Whirlpool Galaxy

Of all the galaxies visible in the sky, this is one of the best to look at, in my opinion. It is not the brightest by any means and is easily beaten by the Andromeda Galaxy on that score, but through a modest-sized telescope the spiral structure of the galaxy is revealed and it is a truly remarkable sight. From a dark site with a moonless sky, its companion galaxy can also be seen. A great example of two galaxies gravitationally interacting.

▶ *The Whirlpool Galaxy reveals its structure even in smaller telescopes.*

10.   The Milky Way

I have left the best to last! Of all the sights in the night sky, the most stunning for me is the combined light from the billions of stars making up our own Galaxy (notice the capitalized 'G' to differentiate it from other galaxies), the Milky Way. Get away from lights and pick a moonless night, and you will be treated to the wonderful view of the Milky Way arching across the sky from horizon to horizon. It takes no optical instruments to fully appreciate it, just your eyes. Give yourself time to explore its many swirls and chains of stars and dark nebulae interrupting the glittering backdrop of stars. It needs no more to be said – utterly beautiful!

◀ *The Milky Way is home to an estimated 400 billion stars.*

Other things to look for

Throughout the year there are plenty of other things to look out for, not just stars, galaxies and nebulae. The planets, too, are of course worth hunting down but, as we have already seen, they move their position relative to the stars so it is not easy to articulate where to find them in a book. You can find their positions easily enough by using either a Philip's planisphere or one of the many apps for smartphones, or online websites and planetarium software. Wherever the planets are, they will always be lurking somewhere along the ecliptic, which is the path that most Solar System objects tend to follow. Keep an eye on the constellations along that path and if there is a bright object where you are not expecting to find one, then the chances are it will be a planet. Planets aside, there are plenty of other things you can look out for.

Spend a few hours under a dark moonless night sky away from city lights and before long you will pick out your first satellite moving silently across the sky. These are easy to differentiate from aircraft, which flash – satellites look just like stars but move with a steady glow. Sometimes they will seem to fade from view, which is when they pass into the shadow cast by the Earth in space. The International Space Station, or ISS,

is a great one to watch out for as it orbits the Earth at an altitude of about 370 km, completing an orbit once every 90 minutes. However, that does not mean we can see it as it passes over every 90 minutes, because it is often lost from view as it is hidden by the shadow of the Earth. NASA has some great resources online to help you identify when and where to look to see it, and it can be a very impressive sight. It is most definitely worth looking out for, and on some of its passes the ISS can shine brighter than any star in the sky and is obvious as it moves silently among the backdrop of stars. Plenty of other satellites can be seen on any night, some quite faint, others a little brighter, but keep your eyes peeled and you will soon spot your first one.

Not only will you see satellites on any night of the year, but you may well also spot the odd meteor or shooting star, to use their more common name. These are

◄ *No equipment is needed to try and spot meteors, but you may need a bit of luck!*

not related in any way to stars but they do resemble them, shooting across the sky as if propelled by some unseen force. In reality, they are tiny pieces of rock hurtling through our atmosphere at speeds in excess of 50 km/sec. As they plummet towards the ground, the gas surrounding them gets compressed, causing them to glow and giving them their trademark appearance. There is a lot of confusion around the terms describing these falling rocks, but the concept is pretty easy to understand: when they are travelling through space they are called *meteoroids*; when they enter our atmosphere but burn up before hitting the ground, they are called *meteors*; and if they survive their fiery plunge to the surface they are known as *meteorites*.

You may be lucky and see the odd meteor on any night of the year – these random one-off events are known as *sporadic*, because they are not attached to any particular meteor shower. However, throughout the year there are about 20 or so meteor showers that are reliably on display the same time each year. The showers are the result of the Earth passing through the orbit of a comet, which is peppered with debris from the comet. As Earth travels through the orbit, it sweeps up the debris in the same way that flies hit the front of your car as you drive through a swarm on a summer's day. From Earth, we see this as a burst of meteor activity that lasts for a couple of weeks either side of the shower's peak, which is driven by the Earth passing through the densest part of the debris field.

During one of these meteor showers, the meteors all seem to come from one point in the sky known as the *radiant*, but this is only due to the effect of perspective. In reality, the meteroids are all hitting the Earth in parallel paths, but in the same way that the parallel lines of a railway track all seem to converge to a point on the horizon, so do the meteors in a meteor shower. Interestingly, the name of the shower is taken from the constellation within which the radiant sits, so the Leonid shower has its radiant in Leo and is the result of Earth passing through the orbit of Comet Tempel–Tuttle. The Earth intersects these cometary orbits at the same time each year, so we see the showers on the same days year after year – the only thing that varies is how many meteors we will see. In an attempt to articulate just how spectacular a meteor shower will be, there is a term called the *zenithal hourly rate*, which defines how many meteors would be visible on a dark moonless night with the radiant sitting directly overhead. Invariably, the conditions are never perfect and with a lower radiant, the light from the Moon interfering, or even your observing location on Earth not being ideally placed, the actual number of meteors seen will be less than the ZHR suggests.

Among the list of 20 or so meteor showers visible each year, my favourites are listed here, but the dates are approximate and may vary by a day or so:

2 January	Quadrantids
21 April	Lyrids
5 May	Eta Aquarids
11/12 August	Perseids
21 October	Orionids
16 November	Leonids
12/13 December	Geminids

To try and see the meteors it is best to be on the forwards-facing side of the Earth when the shower peaks, which happens when the peak of activity occurs just after midnight from your location. This means you will get the best display, but regardless of whether you are lucky enough to be in an optimum location, the early morning hours are always best to try and see meteor showers. Get yourself wrapped up warm and comfortable on a sun lounger or other outside seat and simply look skywards. It is best not to look in the direction of the radiant as the trails from meteors will be quite short and hard to detect, so look in a different direction. I find between 40° and 60° away from the radiant is best and you should get to see quite a few.

If you are diligent enough to get up early or stay up late to catch the peak of a meteor shower, then you may be disappointed to find it is cloudy, but do not worry and do not head for bed – there is another option: you could try and listen to the meteors instead! As the meteors plummet to the Earth they ionize the atoms of gas in their path, leaving a trail of them for a brief moment. The process of ionization refers to an atom of gas gaining or losing some electrons, which means they become either negatively or positively charged. It is possible for our own terrestrial radio signals to bounce off these trails of ionized gas and you can tune in to these reflected radio signals with nothing more than a basic FM radio. A car radio will work perfectly well for this and the trick is to tune in to a station that is about 1,000 km away and one that you would not normally be able to pick up. You can find a suitable one by looking for towns and cities about that distance away from you and then look up a suitable radio station based in that town. Tuning in to a station like this will usually result in hearing a general hissing sound. Doing this during a meteor shower, however, will mean that the transmitted radio signals will get reflected off the ionized trails and bounced back down to Earth. You will either hear the station for a brief moment or maybe even hear pops and whistles as the meteors zip through. It is a great way of trying to observe a shower even if it is cloudy.

There are other transient events going on in the sky and perhaps one of the most spectacular is the aurora. These beautifully enigmatic and almost ghostly displays can be hard to predict and hard to observe if you are further away from the poles of the Earth, but if you do get to see one they can be an amazing sight. An aurora is more properly called *aurora borealis* for northern-hemisphere displays and *aurora australis* for southern-hemisphere displays, but both are the result of the same process. It is not surprising that the Sun kicks out huge amounts of heat and light, but it also gives off a nearly constant stream of electrically charged particles. These particles, which are known as the *solar wind*, rush out from the Sun at around 400 km/sec and when they get to the Earth they slam into our magnetic field.

The magnetic field channels the particles around to the northern and southern magnetic poles of the Earth, where they cascade down into the atmosphere, exciting the atoms in the gas and causing them to glow. The same process is seen inside fluorescent-tube lighting, where electricity causes the gas inside the tube to glow and give off its own light. In the case of the auroral displays, we see different colours because of the different gases in our atmosphere – the green colours come from low-level oxygen, while oxygen at higher altitudes leads to red aurorae. Nitrogen, on the other hand, produces blue light or red/purple, depending on the charge of the gas atoms. We know from records that the activity of the

▲ *Aurorae borealis are easier to see at higher latitudes but the bigger displays can also be seen further south.*

Sun peaks every 11 years, and we can see that not only in the sunspots visible on the solar disk but also in the increase in auroral activity. There are some great online resources which can alert you to possible auroral displays, so keep an eye on them, and if an alert does come in then wrap up warm, get outside and keep an eye on the northern horizon if you live in the northern hemisphere, or on the southern horizon if you live in the southern hemisphere. You will need to make sure that there are no sources of light pollution in the direction you are looking otherwise the displays may get lost in the glow, so it is worth scouting out some possible locations for when an alert comes in. I remember one time not having done this and I found myself on a particularly dark and lonely road in Norfolk called Hanging Hill – not a good place to be on your own in the dead of night, but I did see the most incredible auroral display from there!

We have seen that meteor showers are predictable and that aurorae can be predictable in the short term, but another event to look out for is an eclipse. There are two sorts of eclipses: lunar eclipses, where the Earth passes directly between the Moon and Sun, and thus the Moon falls into Earth's shadow; and solar eclipses, where the Moon passes directly between the Earth and Sun, and so casts a shadow on to the Earth in a very localized spot. Lunar eclipses are the easiest to observe because the eclipsed Moon will be visible from half of the Earth at any one time, and if you can see the Moon you will see the eclipse. You might expect that during lunar eclipses the Moon would go completely dark as no sunlight can get to it and illuminate it, but if you have ever seen an eclipse then you will know that, instead, the Moon turns a deep coppery red – this is because a small amount of sunlight passes through our atmosphere. Essentially, the colours from the violet and blue end of the spectrum get absorbed or filtered out, but the red light passes through and gets diverted or refracted into the shadow zone where the eclipsed Moon sits, gently illuminating it with a red glow. Lunar eclipses from start to finish can take a couple of hours and there are some known as *total eclipses*, where the Moon is totally eclipsed by the Earth, and *partial eclipses*, where only part of the Moon falls into the Earth's shadow. Eclipses of the Moon can be observed with the naked eye or through binoculars, or even through a telescope, but my personal preference is for naked-eye observation as this somehow seems to retain the real beauty of the event, more than magnified observations.

More difficult to observe are solar eclipses, where the Moon blocks sunlight from reaching the Earth. These events are harder to observe simply because you need to be in a very specific location on Earth to be able to see the eclipse. It is easy to understand that you can see the Sun from half of the Earth at any one time, but during solar eclipses the eclipse path is very much more localized, often sweeping out a thin band just a few hundred kilometres across as the eclipse progresses. Just like their lunar counterparts, solar eclipses can be partial when the Moon blocks a portion of the Sun from view, and these events can often pass without anyone even noticing something is going on. The really spectacular event, though, is the *total solar eclipse*, and it is these eclipses that people travel to all corners of the world to try and see. It is just luck that at the moment the Moon and the Sun generally appear the same size in the sky. But the elliptical nature of the Moon's orbit can sometimes mean that the Moon is just a little smaller, and if an eclipse happens at this point then an *annular eclipse* can take place, where the silhouetted Moon is surrounded by a 'ring of fire' from the bright solar disk. Unfortunately, it is a pretty dangerous pursuit to observe a solar eclipse unless you know what you are doing. The only time that it is safe to look directly at the Sun without any filtration or projection techniques is during the total phase of the eclipse, as even just a glimmer of light from the bright disk of the Sun can be enough to cause damage to your eyesight. As you will see in Chapter 7, there are safe ways to observe the

▲ *Lunar eclipses are great to observe with the naked eye and the colour changes can be quite beautiful.*

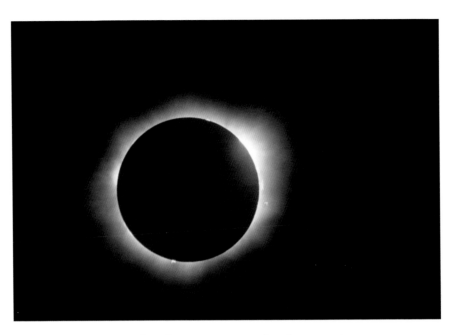

▲ *Solar eclipses are rare but if you get to see one do take precautions to protect your eyes.*

partial phases of an eclipse by either projecting the image from binoculars or a telescope, or by the use of specialist astronomical solar filters. For the brief moment of totality, which only lasts for just a few minutes, usually seven at the most, then you can enjoy the beauty of the event without any optical projection, **but do remember to take great care**. Unfortunately, I have yet to witness a total solar eclipse, although I have experienced a couple. That may sound a silly statement, but it means that I have been to places where a total eclipse was visible but, alas, was thwarted by cloud – although at the moment of totality, everything went dark and it was the most surreal, eerie yet wonderful experience. I cannot wait to actually get to see one for real. During the moment of totality, the bright light from the Sun's disk, known as the photosphere, is no longer visible, allowing you to see the fainter and beautiful wispy features of the Sun's outer atmosphere, called the corona. I am reliably informed it is one of the most amazing sights that Mother Nature has to offer.

Hopefully, by now you have had plenty of opportunity to take in the wonders of the night sky using just your eyes. You may well have picked out some stunning celestial views, started to identify some constellations, maybe seen some meteors or the odd satellite passing by. You might have picked out one of the handful of galaxies visible to the naked eye or some of the multitude of star clusters. If you have visited your local astronomy society then you may even have had a chance to look through some different types of telescopes. Either way, there will soon come a time, if not already, that you will want to get a closer view and will be thinking about buying astronomical equipment, which we will now look at in Chapter 3.

CHOOSING EQUIPMENT

I ALWAYS ADVISE beginners to stay away from a telescope purchase in the first instance, simply because it can lead to frustration. Until you have a feel for the night sky, and also an idea of the things you would like to look at, then you could end up buying a telescope not quite suited to your needs. There is always the slim chance, too, that you will buy a telescope too early, only to find astronomy is not for you after all! Before leaping into the expensive purchase of a telescope it is worth trying out a pair of binoculars first. Binoculars come in many different sizes, but they are all 'classified' using one very simple method which defines how much magnification they produce and also the diameter of the main (or objective) lenses at the front; for example, 7 × 50 binoculars would yield a magnification of 7×, with an objective lens diameter of 50 mm.

One very important concept in binoculars and telescopes, too, is that magnification is not everything – of more importance is light-gathering power and that comes from the size

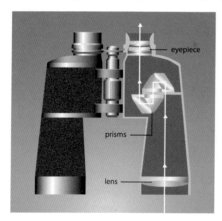

of the main lens. If you think of the lens as a funnel for light (just like a funnel for water), then it is easy to understand that a larger lens will collect more light than a smaller one. The lens brings incoming rays of light to a focus, so larger ones bring more rays of light to a focus and send them into your eye. For binoculars, a larger 'second' number means the main lenses are larger, will collect more light and allow you to see fainter objects. The downside to this is that a larger set of lenses means the binoculars are heavier to hold, but tripods can resolve that issue.

Ideally you would have both, but in

◀ *(top) Most binoculars use a combination of accurately aligned lenses and prisms to form the image. (bottom) Binoculars are great for beginners to learn their way around the sky without having to worry about complicated adjustments that can be found on telescopes.*

▶ *Attaching binoculars to a tripod is a good way to steady the view.*

reality a compromise between light-gathering ability and magnification should be aimed for. Something called 'eye relief' is also important when it comes to using binoculars and we will look at this in more detail in the eyepieces section of Chapter 5 (see page 110). For now, though, it is useful to know that eye relief explains how far the eye needs to be away from the eyepieces of the binoculars in order to see the whole field of view. It is of greater interest if you wear glasses for astigmatism, since you will still need to wear them for viewing. A larger eye relief will allow you to view comfortably while still wearing glasses, whereas eye relief that is too short will mean you will not get to see the full field of view. Too short an eye relief even for those of you without glasses will make viewing uncomfortable, as you have to press your eyes close to the eyepieces.

I started off with, and still use regularly, a pair of 7 × 50 binoculars and they work very nicely for astronomy – they only cost around £20 and were bought from a second-hand shop. It is possible to get much larger binoculars but their cost is usually pretty high, even of the order of thousands of pounds for a quality pair, and with bigger binoculars comes the necessity of putting them on a very sturdy mount. If you go much over 7 × 50, then you might want to think about attaching them to a standard photographer's tripod. It will become obvious when you start using binoculars or telescopes that not only do they magnify distant objects, but they also magnify any movement that you pass on to them through your hands. A sturdy tripod will remove this and give you a much steadier image to enjoy, and you can buy little adaptor blocks to connect the two together.

All that said, it can be rather uncomfortable looking through binoculars on a tripod, particularly if you are gazing overhead, unless, of course, you are a contortionist! A nice addition to a standard tripod is to get a parallelogram binocular mount. These generally bolt on to a normal tripod but they take the binoculars away from the centre of the mount, making overhead use much easier.

▲ *Binoculars on a parallelogram mount are ideal for astronomy and allow you to share your view more easily.*

They also have the added benefit of allowing you to adjust the height for other people to look through without altering where they are pointing – quite a neat piece of engineering and lovely to use.

Image stabilization is a relatively new technology for binoculars, which adds a lot to the price but does work very nicely to steady the image. They cleverly remove any tremors or tiny vibrations that you would normally see from hand-held instruments. If you can afford it, then this is a very good option, although personally I would rather spend money on perhaps a better-quality pair of binoculars with a tripod than cheaper ones with image stabilization.

Binoculars will give you a closer and slightly brighter view of most objects, but with the small magnifications on offer it will not be long before you are longing to buy your own telescope. When looking to buy your first one, and as a newcomer to the world of astronomy, it is all too easy to get lost in the terminology and end up buying something which is not ideal for your use. My first important piece of advice is to steer well clear of any telescope sold in a department store. That might be a sweeping statement, but in my experience telescopes sold in stores like that tend to be of pretty poor quality. Often they will exaggerate their capabilities – for example, I have seen cheap 50 mm telescopes boast a 'space busting' 400× magnification! For any telescope, small or large, good quality or poor, there is a limit to how much useful magnification it can offer you based on the diameter or aperture of its main lens or mirror. A fairly good estimate for this is 50× per 25 mm of aperture, so, in the example, a telescope with a 50 mm lens would only be able to offer a useful magnification of around 100×, and in my opinion that is far from 'space busting'.

A safer approach is to buy a telescope from a specialist supplier, either astronomical or even some of the more reputable photographic stores. Before you can decide which telescope to buy, there are a number of things to consider, but before we can look at these it is necessary to understand a little about telescopes and their mounts. There is a huge range of them on the market, but they all follow pretty standard designs.

▲ *Galileo's telescope was a very basic refracting telescope that magnified objects by a factor of five.*

The type of instrument that everyone thinks of when the word 'telescope' is mentioned is the refracting variety, and it is the sort that you will see sailors using in films as they look out to sea. These were the first telescopes to be invented and it was a Dutch spectacle-maker called Hans Lippershey who discovered he could magnify objects by placing some lenses in certain configurations. The first telescope built by Lippershey, in 1608, magnified a whopping 3×, but a later improved version built by Galileo magnified by 5× and it was he who was the first to turn one to the sky and make all manner of wonderful discoveries. At one end of the telescope tube is a lens which collects incoming starlight and passes it down the tube, bringing it to a point of focus at the far end. This is where the eyepiece is placed which magnifies the focused starlight. There will be more about these later in Chapter 5, but for now it is enough to understand that an eyepiece is a collection of smaller lenses all mounted together in a small tube, which gets inserted into the near end of the tube.

The main or objective lens in a modern good-quality refracting telescope is made up of a number of lenses all mounted together in one supporting cell. We can look at the properties of light for the reason behind this approach. All light travels at 300,000 km/sec and, as we saw in Chapter 1, its 'colour' is determined by a property known as its wavelength. Light from the stars is made up of lots of different wavelengths of light. The property of wavelength can be visualized by imagining a wave on the ocean with the distance between the crest of two successive waves as the wavelength. It is exactly the same for light. As starlight passes through any medium such as air, water or even glass, it gets refracted by an amount dependent on the material refracting it and its wavelength. The effect of this is that the component parts of starlight are not all focused to the same point. If telescopes just had one lens, like the first ones invented over 400 years ago, then they would suffer from a horrible optical effect called *chromatic aberration*. An observer looking through a telescope like this would see an image with multicoloured haloes of light surrounding it, and it would be impossible to get one sharp, perfectly coloured image. This problem is corrected by using more than one lens, shaped to bring all of the incoming starlight to a focus at the same point. This is why good-quality telescopes with lenses are more expensive than other types, because there is a higher manufacturing cost.

The other main type of telescope is the reflecting telescope and it differs by using a mirror to collect incoming starlight rather than a lens. With astronomical telescope mirrors, the front surface has a very precise and accurate curve ground into

▶ *A modern wide-field refracting telescope attached to an altazimuth telescope mount.*

Refracting and reflecting telescopes

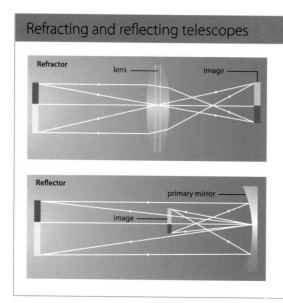

Refracting telescopes (top) were the first type to be invented. Modern versions use a number of lenses to collect incoming light and bring it to a focus.

Reflecting telescopes (bottom) use mirrors to collect incoming light and produce the image. Because the mirrors can be supported at the back, much larger instruments can be made.

it, which is then coated with a highly reflective material. The starlight hits the surface and bounces off, unlike the refractor where the light has to pass through two surfaces for each lens. The best-quality refractor is known as an *apochromatic*, which has at least three lenses making up the 'main' lens, so that means six surfaces to shape accurately. In contrast, the best-quality reflecting telescopes still have only one surface to shape, which is a whole lot easier and cheaper to manufacture. Pound for pound, a reflecting telescope is cheaper when compared to a refracting telescope of the same size.

The optical layout of a reflecting telescope is different to the refractor. The incoming starlight passes straight down the main tube before striking the main or 'primary' mirror, which has the very special curve ground into it. The light bounces back up the tube with the rays of light slowly coming to a focus, but before they do, they hit a second mirror (not surprisingly called the 'secondary' mirror), which is in the centre of the tube at the top and mounted at a 45° angle. This allows the light to be redirected out the side of the tube, where the eyepiece is placed, and the astronomer looks at the resultant image. One reason why the largest telescopes are reflectors rather than refractors is

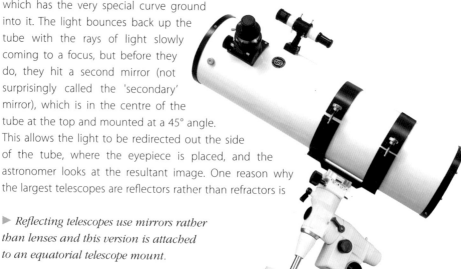

▶ *Reflecting telescopes use mirrors rather than lenses and this version is attached to an equatorial telescope mount.*

due to the way the optics can be mounted. A refracting telescope relies on light passing through the lens so it must be held securely around the edges, unlike a reflecting telescope whose light bounces off the front surface. This design allows the mirror to be supported from the back which means larger chunks of glass can be used, but in a refractor the large lens will start to sag under its own weight. Anything much larger than a metre will suffer image degradation due to the lens warping.

The largest refracting telescope ever made was for the Great Paris Exhibition of 1900 and had a lens of 1.25 m; however, it was impractical in design and never successfully used for astronomical purposes. A slightly smaller telescope was made at 1.02 m and is still in use at the Yerkes Observatory at the University of Chicago. By contrast, the Subaru Telescope on Mauna Kea in Hawai'i has a mirror 8.2 m across, although much larger new telescopes are now being produced that use mirror segments rather than one large mirror. The largest to date is found on the Canary Islands, measuring a total of 10.4 m with 36 individually mounted segments, but this is nothing compared to the proposed and aptly named European Extremely Large Telescope, measuring a whopping 39.3 m across with 798 hexagonal segments, each measuring 1.45 m across.

Catadioptric telescopes are a popular alternative combination of both a reflecting and a refracting telescope and come in many different designs. One of the most popular is the Schmidt-Cassegrain, where starlight first travels through a lens at the front of the telescope, then down the tube to hit a mirror before bouncing back up the tube to hit a second mirror, and finally down the tube for a second time, through a hole in the main mirror and into the eyepiece. These telescopes offer the best of both worlds, with a large aperture for faint objects and long focal length for higher magnifications. The optical design is particularly useful as the length of tube is shortened by the use of the second mirror, which sends the

▲ *The preliminary design for the European Extremely Large Telescope (E-ELT), which will be composed of 798 mirror segments, each one meauring 1.45 metres across.*

Catadioptric telescopes

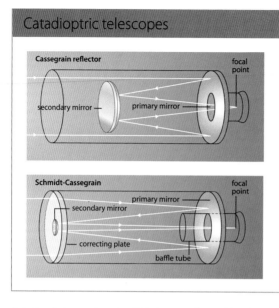

Catadioptric telescopes generally use mirrors and lenses to collect incoming light. One of their common features is the way the optical design utilizes mirrors to 'fold up' the light path, thus giving a long-focal-length telescope a much more manageable short tube.

light back down the tube. This is great for making large telescopes more portable, which is ideal if you need to travel to your observing site. One downside is that the enclosed nature of the tube means the whole system can take a long time to cool down at night, which, as you will see in the next chapter, is key to getting good views.

One of the compromises with this style of telescope is the long focal length, giving a relatively narrow field of view which is not ideal for deep-sky observing. This can be nicely resolved with a 'focal reducer' attached at the eyepiece end of the telescope, which, as the name suggests, turns a longer-focal-length telescope into a shorter one. My telescope is slightly different to the standard Cassegrain design as there is no big lens at the front. Instead, the starlight first strikes the primary mirror before bouncing back up the tube to the secondary mirror, where it passes through a small lens in front before it hits the mirror. The light gets bounced back down the tube and out through a hole in the primary mirror, just like the standard Cassegrain concept. This has the advantage that it is much quicker to cool down, but still has a short tube making it relatively portable. It has a focal length of 3 m, but I use a focal reducer when studying deep-sky objects, which brings the focal length down to a much more manageable 1.8 m.

◀ *SCT telescopes are a popular type of catadioptric telescope that often come with computer control.*

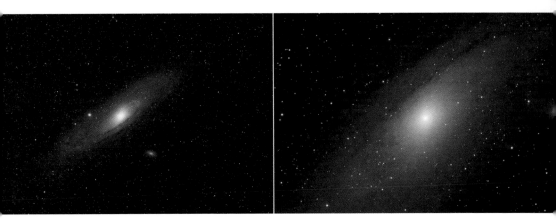

▲ *Telescopes of different aperture and focal lengths will give different views through a telescope. The left image shows M31 through a 10 cm (4-inch) aperture, 50 cm (19-inch) focal-length telescope compared to the right image which shows the same object through a 50 cm (19-inch) diameter, 2.25 m (88-inch) focal-length telescope.*

Already we have looked at a telescope's aperture, which is used to explain the diameter of the main mirror or lens. The larger the aperture, the more light it will collect, allowing you to see fainter objects. A large aperture also allows you to see a finer level of detail than a smaller telescope, which is defined by another new term: resolution, or resolving power. The other important term which defines a telescope is its focal length and it is a concept that has been introduced already. The purpose of a mirror or a lens is to bring incoming beams of light to focus at a point. The distance it takes for those beams to come into focus is called the focal length and, depending on the aperture of the mirror or lens, it can range from around 30 cm for small telescopes up to many metres for larger telescopes. The focal length of a telescope is linked to how much magnification it can produce, with longer focal lengths able to produce higher magnifications than shorter focal lengths. Magnification is found by dividing the focal length of the telescope by the focal length of the eyepiece, so by changing the eyepiece, you can change the magnification. One of the side effects of higher magnifications is that the resultant image will be darker than a lower magnification. This is why the aperture of a telescope will limit how much it can magnify because of the amount of available light. A good example is that cheap little telescope I saw in the department store with 50 mm aperture and a focal length of 1,000 mm. With the eyepieces supplied and a focal length of 1,000 mm, it certainly could produce a magnification of 400×, *but* because it only has an aperture of 50 mm, the image would be so dark that it would be barely visible.

Another indication of the way a telescope will perform is given by its focal ratio, which is written as f/ratio and spoken as 'ef ratio'. The f/ratio of any telescope is calculated by dividing the focal length by the aperture, so my telescope, which has a focal length of 3,000 mm and an aperture of 260 mm, has an f/ratio of f/11.5. Anyone who has photographic experience will recognize this term, which is also used to describe the 'speed' of a lens: a higher f/ratio means a slower lens and a lower f/ratio means a faster lens.

▶ *Finder telescopes make locating objects significantly easier.*

Describing f/ratio in terms of speed has its origins in photography as it relates to the relative length of exposure driven by the brightness of the image produced by the lens. A higher f/ratio means a darker image and a longer exposure, so the lens would be described as slow. The same terms are used in astronomy and provide a guide to the brightness of the image. This is not only useful when considering astronomical photographs, but also the suitability of a telescope to a particular object. Faster telescopes (lower f/ratio) mean brighter images, so they are more suited to fainter objects like galaxies and nebulae, whereas slower telescopes with higher f/ratios are more suited to brighter objects like the planets and the Moon.

Attached to the side of the main telescope is a smaller refracting telescope known as the finder telescope. These are essential for tracking down objects and you really cannot be without one. The area of sky or field of view that your telescope shows you will be very small and trying to home in on a planet or galaxy is difficult. It is a bit like looking through a cardboard tube and trying to walk around your home, not that I suggest you try that now, but it is easy to see how it would be difficult as you would soon bump into things! Navigating the sky through a telescope is tricky, so instead the finder telescope offers you a much greater view of the sky, making it much easier to line up the main telescope.

Key to the performance of a telescope, though, is the mount upon which is sits. There are two main types of telescope mount: the *altazimuth* mount and the *equatorial* mount. The altazimuth mount is not too dissimilar to a photographic tripod, having two axes about which the telescope moves. This type of mount gets its name from the celestial co-ordinates we looked at in Chapter 1: altitude and azimuth. As you will remember, altitude refers to height above the horizon and azimuth refers to distance around the horizon from the north. One of the axes of the altazimuth mount pivots to move the telescope up and down, while the other axis pivots to move the telescope around the horizon. Using this, you can point

◀ *Altazimuth telescope mounts are easy to use and great for beginners.*

the telescope at all parts of the sky, although it does make it tricky to look through it when pointing overhead. These mounts are great and really easy to use – they can even have motors attached to the two axes to enable them to follow objects automatically across the sky as they rise in the east and set in the west. It is necessary to have a motor on each axis because objects get higher in the sky (increase in altitude) as they rise in the east before getting lower again in the west, and slowly move around the sky towards the west. It takes some pretty complicated electronics to control these motors but they are readily available on many amateur telescopes. Other versions of the mount might have long bendy rods known as *slow-motion controls*, which are attached to gears on the two axes. These allow you to make very fine adjustments to where the telescope is pointing, much finer than you could do by hand alone.

Altazimuth or altaz mounts, as they are often called, do have one major drawback which is much more of an issue if you want to take photographs through the telescope. You can see what these might be if you look at the Moon next time it rises in the east. Notice the orientation of the Moon against the horizon and then look a good few hours later when it is over near the western horizon. The sharp-eyed amongst you will realize that it seems to have rotated in the sky! This rotation of an object in the sky is even more noticeable if you look at it through a telescope. Over the course of one night the Moon, and all other astronomical objects, will slowly rotate when viewed through the eyepiece of a telescope. This is no real problem if you are just looking at them, but if you would like to try and get a photograph of them then somehow you need to get rid of the image rotation, otherwise you will get blurred images. Many of the large professional telescopes use altazimuth mounts and to get rid of the rotating image they use devices known, rather imaginatively, as *field derotators*. They fit to the end of the telescope where the camera sits and slowly rotate to compensate for the rotation of the object.

Another way of resolving the issue of a rotating image is to use an equatorial tele-scope mount instead. This type of mount is essential for astronomical imaging and works by aligning the mount with the rotation of the Earth. In Chapter 1 we looked at the north celestial pole and how the axis of rotation of the Earth points in that direction. Equatorial mounts differ from altazimuth mounts by tilting it so that one of the axes is pointing at the north celestial pole for northern hemisphere observers, and the south celestial

◄ *An equatorial telescope mount is essential for counteracting the rotation of the Earth and taking sharp astronomical pictures.*

▶ *There are a few types of equatorial mount but the German equatorial mount shown here is one of the more popular designs.*

pole for the southern hemisphere. The axis which points towards the celestial pole is known as the polar axis, and the angle of its tilt from horizontal is equal to the latitude of your location. The polar axis of my telescope is set to 52°, which is the same as my latitude in the UK. The alignment of this *polar axis* is critical in astronomical imaging, but this is all covered in Chapter 4. By attaching a motor to the polar axis, the telescope can now be turned at the same speed as the Earth's rotation, but in the opposite direction to keep objects in the eyepiece or on the camera chip. The beauty of this design is that the tilting of the polar axis makes the telescope naturally follow an arc, climbing and descending as it moves around the sky, mimicking the rotation of the image.

The equatorial or the altazimuth part of the telescope mount is often referred to as the *head*, and it attaches to the top of either a tripod or a single pillar with feet at the bottom. Whichever mounting approach you end up with, it is crucially important that it is well built and stable. A cheap wobbly mount will render your telescope almost unusable, so make sure you invest in a good one.

Now comes the hard bit: choosing the right telescope for you. You have your hard-earned cash and now want to buy your first shiny new telescope. By now you may find yourself leaning towards a particular branch of astronomy – perhaps you find the planets fascinating or are totally absorbed in the wonders of deep space. Your area of interest is one of the factors to consider when making your choice, but there are plenty of other things to think about. First things first, buy from a reputable astronomy dealer to be sure you are getting good quality. I have seen plenty of cheap telescopes on the market which have horrible plastic lenses, wobbly tripods or overinflated promises of high magnification. If you have hooked up with your local astronomy society by now, then you may well find some good second-hand deals to be had from amongst their membership. This is a pretty safe source of second-hand equipment of good quality, as you are very unlikely to find a member selling equipment to another member if it is of questionable worth. The monthly magazines are a good source for second-hand equipment too, but you really need to know what you are looking at before parting with your money on an unknown piece of kit. You will generally be able to find someone in your society who knows the reputable members of the astronomy community, so you can always ask them for advice if you are going down the second-hand route. Be warned, though – a telescope may appear to have been well maintained, but a sure-fire way of making sure the optics are in good condition is to take a look through it at some stars at night using a moderately high magnification. A general rule of thumb is that good telescopes produce nice pinpoint star images, while bad telescopes produce funny-shaped star images. Of course, the eyepiece can affect this significantly, but if it is a second-hand telescope of unknown origin and you do not know the seller, then steer clear if the stars are not sharp. There is always the risk that the optics on a brand-new telescope may not be of good quality, but most suppliers are pretty reasonable if there is a problem. Whether you buy new or second-hand will be determined quite a lot by the budget you have available. If you are looking for a new entry-level telescope then you should expect to spend anything from around £200, and second-hand instruments are likely to start at around £100.

Another option to consider, although it is less popular than it once was, is still a great route if you enjoy making things and that is to build your own telescope. The mechanics of the telescope tube itself are pretty basic and just have to offer some way of holding the optics securely in place while allowing for tiny adjustments to align them. Even the optics can be made yourself – indeed, when I started out in astronomy I built a 15 cm reflecting telescope and ground the mirror myself, too. Mirror kits can still be bought that include everything you need including two glass disks, one which will become the mirror and the other which becomes the 'tool'. The principle is simple and involves rubbing the two disks against each other in a specific way with varying sizes of grit or carborundum between them. After quite a few hours of mirror grinding, this eventually puts a concave curve into the mirror and a convex curve into the tool. The mirror is then polished to produce a curved surface (called a parabola) and a fine smooth finish, before being coated with a highly reflective material. The main mirror and secondary, along with the eyepiece holder, are then all mounted inside the telescope tube and fitted on top of the telescope mount.

Once you have decided on budget – new, second-hand, or even to embark on building your telescope – it is time to start grappling with the multitude of different options. With time, many astronomers lean towards planetary astronomy or deep-sky astronomy, which

encompasses the galaxies, star clusters, and gas clouds known as nebulae. If you still have a very general interest, then your best option is to look for a 15 cm Dobsonian reflector. The diameter of the main mirror is 15 cm and you can get them in a range of different focal lengths or focal ratios, but my recommendation is to look for something that is around f/7 and has a focal length of around 1 m. By choosing a reflector rather

▶ *Telescope mirrors are ground out of two glass disks.*

than a refractor, you are getting the most aperture for your money, otherwise the same amount of money spent on a refractor would perhaps only get you a telescope half the size. A 15 cm telescope will allow you to push magnifications up to around 300✕, which is excellent for planetary work, and the aperture will allow you to see objects down to magnitude 14 under dark skies (1,500 times fainter than the objects visible to the naked eye). The term 'Dobsonian' refers to the style of mount, which is based on the altazimuth concept. The design is simple, very easy to use and set up, and easily portable so you can transport it to different observing locations should you need to. This is really important if you live in a town or city and want to take your telescope out into the dark of the countryside. The telescope is usually mounted in nothing more than a box around its middle, with two bearings fitted either side. The telescope then sits on top of another box, with the bearings giving it the ability to move up and down and change the altitude that the telescope is pointing at. The whole lot is then fitted to a base plate, which is usually circular or square and against which the main box can pivot, giving the telescope its motion in azimuth around the horizon. They are very easy to move around the sky, which makes the design excellent for newcomers.

Of all the mounts you can buy, there are about three really common types. The Dobsonian is an altazimuth mount, and is very similar to the fork mount where the telescope pivots between two vertical posts, with the whole lot swivelling around a vertical axis. Fork mounts are often found in an equatorial design too, where the vertical axis is tilted over to point in the same direction as the rotational axis of the Earth. Another very popular type of equatorial telescope uses the German equatorial mount, where the two axes form a 'T' shape with the upright of the 'T' being aligned to the Earth's axis of rotation, the telescope fitted to one end of the bar of the 'T' and a set of weights to offer a counterbalance to it. These can feel a little hard to use as the axes are often not where you expect them when observing at night, and moving them can take a bit of practice. These are great mounts, however, and it is this sort that I now use.

The only disadvantage with the Dobsonian type of telescope is that you need to know how to find things. The learning process that goes with finding objects in the sky is an invaluable one, though. My knowledge of the sky has been built up over many years of manually finding things with telescopes like these. Without that experience, I would be clueless about

▶ *A Dobsonian reflector telescope is the best value for money for newcomers to astronomy.*

▶ *A computerized telescope takes the hassle out of finding objects in the sky.*

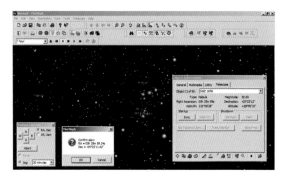

where things are in the sky. The telescope I now use is computer controlled, which allows me to just select an object and the telescope will move to point at it. This is a luxurious state to be in as it saves me lots of time trying to home in on objects, but the process of learning how to find things is well worth going through, albeit frustrating at times.

Over the last few years, the telescope market has been flooded with these computerized mounts, which have the necessary electronics to point the telescope automatically at any object you wish to look at. These are referred to as Go To telescopes by virtue of the fact that they will 'go to' the objects for you. There are other less advanced systems that provide a digital readout to guide you around the sky to the objects. It is possible to get systems that can be retrofitted to your Dobsonian telescope should you wish to add this on later, although they generally cost more than entry-level telescopes, so if you are looking for something like this then it may be better to get a telescope with that feature.

Another serious consideration is whether you are interested in taking images of the night sky. If you are, then a Dobsonian telescope will not provide you with the necessary features for long exposures. As we saw earlier in the chapter, an equatorial mount is needed to combat field rotation, and while it is possible – tricky, but possible – to get images of planets through Dobsonian telescopes, an equatorially driven telescope is by far the best option. As with the Go To systems which can be retrofitted, it is perfectly plausible to buy a Dobsonian telescope first and then take the telescope off its mount and replace it with an equatorial mount at some later date.

Starting with a Dobsonian telescope is great for general observation, but if you have a little more budget and if you already feel yourself leaning towards certain aspects of astronomy then there may be alternative options for you. If you find yourself getting a real buzz from finding faint fuzzy objects in the realm of the deep sky, then I would still stick with a Dobsonian design but go for as large a telescope as you can afford *and* physically handle. A good friend of mine used to own a 50 cm (20-inch diameter) Dobsonian telescope, but it took two people to set it up, he had to use a van to transport it, and needed a tall step-ladder to look through it when he was looking straight up, as it stood about 2.5 m tall! He has sold it now as it was a monster and a pain to set up and use, but it nicely illustrates the fact that the best telescope for you is the one that you use most often. If it takes too much effort to set up, then chances are you won't use it as much as you would if it was easier to handle. If deep-sky observing is your thing, go for aperture to collect as much light as possible, allowing you to see as faint as possible.

On the other hand, if brighter objects like the planets are more your bag, then because the objects you are looking at tend to be brighter, aperture is not so important. Of course, there

◀ *Large Dobsonian telescopes are great light buckets for revealing faint deep-sky wonders.*

is the benefit of resolution or seeing finer levels of detail with a larger telescope, but do not forget that the stability in the atmosphere will limit resolution too. A greater focal length is more beneficial in a planetary telescope so you can push the magnification higher, something which is not so crucial in the fainter objects. For a planetary telescope I would lean more towards a refractor of 10 cm aperture or more, or perhaps even a catadioptric telescope with an aperture of 15 cm or more. The prices will be higher than for the reflector Dobsonian, though, so be sure you really want to concentrate on planetary objects before making a purchase like that. Throughout any amateur astronomer's life, it is very likely that more than one type of telescope will be owned. Some friends of mine have more than one telescope for different objects – others have started with a Dobsonian, sold it and moved on to other telescopes as their interests have evolved.

My own choice of telescope has changed significantly over the 30 or so years that I have studied astronomy. I started off as a youngster about ten years old with a cheap second-hand telescope that I wouldn't now touch with a barge pole! It cost about £20 yet still allowed me to see the Moon and the odd planet, but that was about all I could find with it. It was enough to inspire me to continue with my love of the night sky, though, so a few years later I tried my hand at grinding a 15 cm mirror for a reflecting telescope – it worked but was a bit rudimentary in construction. I then bought a 35 cm mirror and tried (emphasis on the word 'tried') to make a telescope around it. It was not very successful so I started down the route of buying telescopes made properly! The first of these was for the 35 cm mirror, which was fine yet a little unwieldy. I then bought a more portable 20 cm reflecting telescope, motorized and on an equatorial mount. I tried my hand at imaging with this and had pretty good results, although limited by the complexities of film photography. This was soon followed by a Meade LX200 on top of the standard equatorial fork mount, which was an all-singing, all-dancing, computerized telescope and had an aperture of 250 mm. This eventually got upgraded to a 350 mm equivalent, all computerized, but it was far too heavy to use as a portable instrument. I even upgraded the mount for it but the telescope was just a little too heavy for the mount, so I changed to a 150 mm refracting telescope before settling on my current instrument, a 260 mm telescope on a German equatorial mount. My personal interest is in imaging deep-sky objects; however, with my work I need great levels of flexibility, so I actually have two telescopes attached to the mount – the 260 mm is accompanied by a much smaller 80 mm wide-field refractor. These two telescopes mean I have a great combination of focal lengths to allow me to image any object in the sky.

If you have no particular interest at the moment and are looking to spend a little more money on a telescope suited to all objects, then perhaps the larger aperture catadioptric telescopes would be best for you. Their large aperture makes them great for deep-sky objects but their long focal lengths work well for the planets. As we have seen, it is possible to use a focal reducer to reduce the focal length and make the telescope more adept at deep-sky observing, but by removing the focal reducer it is ready for planetary work. These telescopes are great all-rounders but they can be expensive. If you want to invest in one of these, you are better aiming for something around 20 cm aperture or greater to really benefit from their large size.

It is important to make a point here. Although I am recommending different telescopes for planetary and high-resolution astronomy compared to deep-sky observation, a 15 cm f/7 Dobsonian reflector will still give you great images of both – you will just see a little more with something better suited. It is far better to spend a few hundred pounds first and dip your toes in the water before spending many hundreds or even thousands of pounds on something a little more specialist.

Telescope mounts and Go To systems have been covered already, but it is appropriate to say a few words here about telescope drive systems. As you have seen, equatorial telescopes just need the drive to be attached to one axis of the telescope, the polar axis. If the polar axis is pointed perfectly at the celestial pole and the axis turned at a rate of one revolution every 23 hours 56 minutes and 4 seconds, then in theory any object the telescope is pointing at should still be in the centre of the eyepiece hours later. For visual observations this is achievable, but in reality it is unlikely that you will be looking at the same object for hours on end. For that reason, it is not imperative to have a high-quality drive system for visual observing. There are many available mounts on the market that have simple motor drive systems that turn the polar axis to follow objects across the sky.

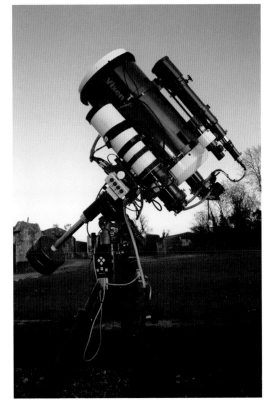

▶ *Author's telescope set-up with a 260 mm Maksutov-Cassegrain and an 80 mm wide-field refractor.*

If you wish to take images of the night sky, then you can get away with one motor if you are taking shots of the planets or the Moon, but if you want to record deep-sky objects you will definitely need a motor attached to the other axis of the telescope as well. This is covered in much more depth in my book *Philip's Astrophotography with Mark Thompson*. If you are thinking of embarking down the astronomical imaging route, be warned – it is not a case of slapping a camera on the telescope and off you go. Planetary imaging is easier than deep sky and requires less equipment, but be prepared for frustrations along the way. However, my other book will help guide you through this journey.

The second motor described above serves a slightly different function than the motor on the polar axis, since it does not turn constantly. The principle is that all mechanical devices are imperfect, and unless you spend a lot of time on it, your polar alignment will also not be perfect. When taking longer-exposure images of the sky, the object must stay in exactly the same position on the camera chip – it can move a few fractions of a millimetre at most, otherwise you will get a blurry image. The process of taking a picture involves you or your computer sending commands to your telescope to tweak the movement of the motors to ensure the object does not move. This will mean slowing or speeding up the polar axis or RA motor, and making the declination motor turn forwards or backwards as appropriate to keep the object centred. If you are thinking about astronomical imaging in the future, then this will be the kind of mount and motor system you will need, but good-quality ones can cost in excess of £500 just for the mount.

You might feel a little daunted by the choices available, so I have broken down all of the options and questions you need to ask yourself in my 'telescope decision maker' opposite, to help you make that all-important decision. If you seek out advice from other people, perhaps members of your local astronomy society, you will be surprised how wide and varied

▲ *The rotation of the Earth causes everything in the night sky to appear to move in a circle around Polaris (centre left), which remains almost stationary.*

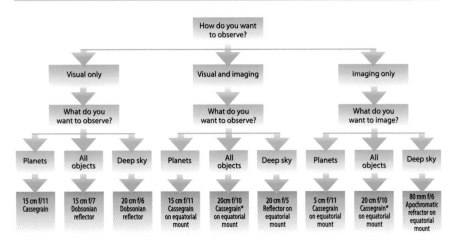

Mark's telescope decision maker

Please note that these are suggestions and only a guide. Choose a telescope that is similar to the specifications above and you will not be disappointed. If cost is an issue, choose a smaller telescope of better quality rather than a larger, poorer quality one.
*Use a focal reducer to facilitate deep-sky imaging

the advice will be. Generally, the variation will be about brands and model numbers rather than types of telescope. I have deliberately restricted my telescope chooser to types of telescope, so as long as you stick to that as a guide and choose a telescope within your budget, you should not be disappointed.

You may have picked up from all of this that there isn't one telescope that fits all your needs. As your interests develop, you may find yourself changing telescopes or mounts a few times until you settle on the ideal system for you. The right telescope will be the one you use most often. Don't forget, the journey you are embarking on is one of enjoying and learning about the night sky, not about telescopes! They are just a means to an end, so whatever telescope you end up going for, it needs to be one that you enjoy using and setting up. You should also consider this: if you are observing in your back garden you may go for a larger telescope than if you are having to transport all of your equipment to an observing site. A big expensive and complicated one may be great, but if you can't be bothered to set it up on a clear night, then it is clearly the wrong one for you. Take your time, look through and try out as many as possible, and I am sure you will make a great choice, one that will open up a window on the Universe for you to enjoy for many years to come.

chapter 4

USING ASTRONOMICAL EQUIPMENT – THE EASY WAY

I F YOU HAVE made it to this chapter, then you are well on your way to uncovering some truly amazing sights in the night sky. You have probably made that all-important choice of a telescope – maybe you, like me, had it out of the box on day one, ignored the instructions and started fiddling with it! That is a good thing to do – unless you break something, in which case it is a bad thing to do, so take care with it! My first proper shop-bought telescope was a fully computerized one and, to be honest, I was at the time reasonably clueless on how to use it. I even remember impatiently firing it up in the lounge in the afternoon and asking it to point at the Orion Nebula for me, which I knew was above the horizon, but instead it reported 'below horizon' with a very condescending beep! Lesson number one: remember to set latitude and longitude, and also remember that it still will not work without having first aligned it with a couple of stars! Anyway, like me, you are now the proud owner of a piece of precisely engineered scientific equipment, possibly the world's most popular at that. But whatever type of telescope you decided upon and whatever your direction of astronomical interest, there are a few things you are going to need to know in order to get the most out of your telescope.

With an astronomical telescope, the tasks to perform while using it can be broken down into two categories: maintenance and operational. Maintenance tasks are those which you need to perform to make sure the telescope is in good working order, whereas operational tasks are those which you will perform during, before or after an observing session. It feels appropriate to cover the operational activities first, because I guarantee you are probably champing at the bit to get set up and looking at the sky. If you have already had 'first light', then hopefully these tips will help you get more out of future sessions.

Set up early!

Something that can affect the performance of your telescope and one of the blights of the astronomer are tube currents. Telescope tubes are generally solid, although many of the larger instruments are now made in some skeletal way with an open tube, which helps to minimize the effects of the currents. Many people leave their telescope indoors, sat in a warm storage place during the day, so it slowly warms. Take it outside into the cold night air for your night of observing and the whole thing becomes a huge radiator of heat. The heat stored up during the day then tries to escape to the atmosphere, and as it tries to escape it gets funnelled out of the tube, producing a hideous distortion of the faint light from the night sky. Open tubes still suffer with this, but, due to their open nature, the heat dissipates quicker

▲ *Setting up early reduces tube currents, giving a sharper image (left) compared with an image taken without giving the tube a chance to cool down (right).*

and the whole set-up reaches the same temperature as the surrounding area much faster. If you look through a telescope suffering with tube currents you will see a very turbulent view, as if the light is being knocked around by some unknown force. I should add here that you would see very similar effects if the atmosphere itself is very turbulent, but more on that later.

Another consequence of taking a warm telescope out into the cold night air is that it could very easily suddenly become covered in dew, and that includes your precious light-collecting mirrors and lenses. The solution to both of these problems is to take your telescope out early and let it cool down before the ambient surrounding air temperature drops too low. Tube currents will dissipate given some time, depending on the conditions, but once your telescope is dewed up you have only a couple of options. Dew on the telescope tube and mount is of no real importance – leave it or wipe it off gently if you prefer, taking care not to scratch your shiny telescope, but I personally would leave it. I was once out until the early hours when the temperature had plummeted to −10°C. The result: a telescope covered in frost, but the optics were kept clear because I had anticipated the low temperatures and prepared my dew-control system accordingly.

Of the two solutions for dew control, my preference is to employ a dew strap, which wraps around the circumference of the optics, gently warming them. The dew strap is electric and the more advanced ones can be set to a particular temperature based on the conditions. Ideally, they are left in place for the duration of the observing session and keep the temperature of the optics just

▶ *A dew-covered lens or mirror is one of the blights of astronomy. Early set-up can reduce this, as can 'dew zappers'.*

above dewpoint to stop the formation of dew. The alternative is less efficient and involves gently blowing warm air on to the optics with a hair dryer to evaporate the water drops. This should ideally be a 12-volt hair dryer powered from a car battery rather than a mains-powered one, given that the conditions are damp. Whatever you do, **do not** get a cloth and wipe your optics until they are free from dew. If there are bits of dust or other contaminants on the surface of the mirror or lens, you will have just wiped them all over the surface, quite likely scratching it, significantly affecting its ability to produce a nice sharp image.

One other reason for setting your telescope up before nightfall, except of course that it is a whole lot easier when you can see what you are doing, is to give the optics a chance to cool down and settle. Warm mirrors and lenses will have slightly different optical properties than cool ones, so giving them a chance to cool down will make them work to their optimum and save you effort later on. This is particularly important when taking images, because although you may have the camera nicely focused at the start of the imaging run, by the time you finish the optics may have cooled more, which will affect the focus of the camera. Result: slightly out-of-focus pictures!

Finder telescope alignment

Finding anything through a telescope is sometimes a frustrating job, but trying without a finder telescope makes it almost impossible. By the nature of their design, telescopes have a very narrow field of view on the sky. I have a 10 mm eyepiece which, with my telescope, gives a field of view on the sky that is about a quarter the size of the full Moon. Trying to home in on a target with such a small view of the sky is really difficult. Attaching a smaller telescope with a much wider field of view to the side of the main instrument will make finding things so much easier. My finder telescope has a field of view that is about 12 times the size of the full Moon, so compared to the narrow view through the eyepiece this makes finding things a whole lot easier.

The principle is that the finder telescope must be aligned to point in exactly the same direction as the main telescope, so that when you are looking for an object, you centre it (or its location – many objects cannot be seen through finder telescopes so you have to identify their location by using patterns of stars) in the finder telescope and it should appear in the centre of the main telescope view.

◀ *A finder telescope is adjusted by turning the tiny screws that hold it in place. The first time you do this, it is best done during daylight using a distant chimney or building to line up on.*

It all sounds too easy, I know, but there is a trick to getting the two telescopes pointing in the same direction. The finder telescope is usually bolted to the side of the main telescope tube and has tiny little screws that will allow you to adjust the direction it is pointing relative to the main telescope. Put a low-power eyepiece (one with a long focal length, 20 mm or more – see Chapter 5) in the telescope and during daytime point it at a chimney or other easily identifiable target. Now look through the finder telescope to see where the chimney appears and adjust the screws on its bracket to bring the chimney to the centre. To fine-tune the alignment and without moving the telescope, change the lower-power eyepiece for a higher-power eyepiece which has a shorter focal length, recentre the chimney and check back through the finder. You will probably find a tiny adjustment is needed to align the two perfectly. Now that you have done this, you can start hunting around the sky for your target with the finder telescope and only when you have located it, or where it should be, will it appear in the main telescope.

Unless your telescope is set up permanently in an observatory, you will have to check this every time you set up for a night's observing. The tiniest knock can push it out of alignment, but with a bit of practice you can complete it in just a few minutes. It is possible to do all this at night using stars or the Moon as alignment objects, but it is made difficult by the fact that the Earth is spinning, making objects move across the sky. If you try this and take too long fiddling with the finder to get the object centred, then by time you are finished the main telescope will not be pointing at it anymore, so you will have got nowhere. You can always use Polaris, the Pole Star, for this as it remains pretty stationary all night, although I find it much easier to stick to this as a daytime activity.

There is a different type of finder telescope which does not actually look like a telescope and is referred to as a *red-dot finder*. Instead of offering a magnified view of the sky, this presents you with a tiny window through which you view the sky, upon which is projected a tiny red dot of light. The red dot is the point of reference where you centre objects. The principle is the same when aligning these devices, but this must be done at night so you can see the red dot.

Polar alignment

Polar alignment is a phrase that sends shivers down the spine of any newcomer to astronomy and even some experienced astronomers. It refers to the act of aligning one of the axes of the telescope, the polar axis, so that it points in exactly the same direction as the axis that the Earth revolves around. The reason why this is useful is that

▲ *Polar alignment is the act of aligning the polar axis of the telescope to the Earth's axis of rotation.*

it makes following objects across the sky much easier. It is nice to have for visual observing, but is essential for astronomical imaging. Once a telescope is polar aligned and an object centred in the eyepiece, then assuming a motor is attached to the telescope, the object will stay centred – and the better the polar alignment, the longer it will stay there. If no motor is attached, then simply nudging the telescope around one axis only will bring the object back to the centre of the eyepiece once again.

Altazimuth telescopes cannot be polar aligned so this is a task only for telescopes fitted to an equatorial mount. As you will recall from Chapter 3, the equatorial mount has two axes and the whole lot is tilted at an angle that equates to your latitude. The result of this tilting is that one of the axes will be pointing in exactly the same direction as the Earth's axis of rotation, and it is the alignment of these two axes that polar alignment refers to.

There are two steps in polar alignment: *rough polar alignment*, which is fine for visual work, and *precise polar alignment*, which is essential to make imaging easy and stress free. Before starting, be sure that your finder telescope is aligned to the main telescope, as explained in the previous section (see page 96).

The objective of rough polar alignment is to get the mount set up so that its polar axis is approximately parallel to the axis of the Earth. This is generally enough for visual work, but is also a necessary step to make the precise polar alignment phase easier. The first step is to adjust the angle of the whole mount so that it is the same as your latitude, and, for that, equatorial mounts have a latitude scale. I live in the UK and my latitude is about 52°, so I would set the latitude to be 52. This is usually done by loosening a nut of some description to allow you to adjust the angle gently before tightening it again. I wholeheartedly recommend doing this without the telescope in place, otherwise you risk the whole lot crashing down. You then have to get the polar axis pointing north, so if you do not know where north is from your observing site, use a compass or smartphone, identify north and point the polar axis in that direction. Alternatively, note the direction of the setting Sun and north is 90° to the right. You should be able to look at the mount now and see that the polar axis is pointing about the same angle above the horizon as your latitude. Mine points just over halfway between the horizon and overhead, which is about right for 52° latitude. Now identify your telescope's declination axis, which is the one with degrees marked all the way around it from 0° to 90°. Rotate the telescope about this axis until it is at 90°. It should now be pointing along the polar axis. Do not worry if you cannot find any degree markings – just turn the telescope so that it is pointing along the polar axis. Your telescope should be reasonably well set up now to get roughly polar aligned.

Identify Polaris, the Pole Star, which is easy to find by following the two pointer stars in the bowl of the Plough, part of the constellation Ursa Major. Now move the entire telescope mount, telescope and all, so that the tube is pointing towards Polaris – this should not need moving much if you pointed it due north using a compass. If you have set up the mount as described above, then Polaris should be visible in the field of view of the finder telescope. Now you just need to make minor adjustments to the mount by fine-tuning its left–right position and your latitude setting to centre Polaris. Assuming your finder telescope is aligned well, you should now see Polaris in the field of view of an eyepiece. Now make tiny adjustments to the mount as before to centre it in the field of view of the

▶ *Polar scopes are found in many telescopes that aid polar alignment.*

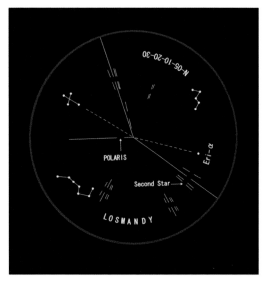

main telescope eyepiece. Your telescope is now roughly polar aligned and will be fine for visual observing. If you are hoping to take images through your telescope, then you will need to move on to precise polar alignment. But if visual is the key, don't waste your time on the next step – just start enjoying the sky.

Some telescopes have polar scopes which are fitted inside the polar axis of the telescope, and they can be a great aid to polar alignment. Looking through a polar scope having completed the steps just outlined will present you with a slightly magnified image of the sky through which the stars are visible. You will also be able to see some lines illuminated gently by a red light. These lines act as a guide to getting a slightly more accurate alignment. In most polar scopes, the illuminated lines in the field of view represent the constellations Cassiopeia, Ursa Minor and Ursa Major, and the polar scope needs to be rotated so the constellations' lines represent the orientation of the constellations in the sky. This is easiest to achieve by keeping both eyes open as you look through the polar scope and adjust it. This has now set up the polar scope correctly for the current time, so all that is needed is to adjust the pointing of the mount, as above, until Polaris sits between the reference lines for it. The previous process of rough polar alignment does not take into account that Polaris sits slightly away from the north celestial pole, but the polar scope does account for this so it actually aligns your mount to the pole, rather than Polaris. This will give you a more accurate degree of polar alignment, but the next stage is necessary for very accurate polar alignment.

The first time you accurately polar align a telescope you should expect to spend an hour or two fiddling around, but eventually you will soon get it down to a fine art. Time spent here is very worthwhile and the benefits will be apparent when it comes to processing your final images. The technique relies on watching the drift of stars through the eyepiece and slowly fine-tuning your polar alignment until there is no drift.

You need an extra piece of equipment to perform this task: an illuminated reticule eyepiece. This is an eyepiece that has either a cross etched into the lens or thin wires forming a cross. These are then illuminated by a faint bulb fitted into the side of the eyepiece. They can be bought from most astronomical suppliers and are essential to the task.

To start polar alignment, identify a star that is roughly due south, or preferably a little to the left of due south and within 5° declination from the celestial equator (the celestial equator is the extension on to the sky of our own Equator and can be seen on any star chart – see diagram on page 20). Centre this star in the field of view of the telescope so that it lies on the illuminated cross. Now, using the slow-motion controls of the telescope, move it east and west in right ascension and rotate the illuminated eyepiece so that one axis of the cross follows that line and the star moves slowly back and forth along it. With the motor running, observe how the star moves, ignoring any left–right movement, just looking at up-and-down drift.

- If it moves down, the polar axis of the telescope is too far to the west (to the left of Polaris).
- If it moves up, the polar axis of the telescope is too far to the east (to the right of Polaris).

Using the mount's azimuth adjustments, make appropriate changes to correct. Now recentre the star and perform the same step again. It will take a few goes, but eventually there will be zero drift up or down for a good five minutes or more.

Now find a star near the eastern horizon; ideally, it should be about 20° above the horizon and fairly close to the celestial equator. Centre it on the cross like before and align the cross so that east–west right ascension movement takes the star along one axis of the cross. Now monitor the star with the motor still running.

- If it drifts down, the polar axis of the telescope is too low.
- If it drifts up, the polar axis of the telescope is too high.

If you do not have a good eastern horizon, a star on the western horizon will work fine, but the notes above regarding adjustments required will need to be swapped.

Make adjustments to the elevation of the polar axis as appropriate, recentre the star and check the drift again. Once drift is eliminated, go back and check with the star due south – once that has been rechecked, your telescope will be accurately polar aligned and objects will stay in the centre of the eyepiece or, more importantly, your camera.

Take the time to really nail this and get your telescope accurately polar aligned, and with some practice you will achieve alignment with quite surprising accuracy. If you want to increase the accuracy further then you can insert a Barlow lens, which doubles or triples the magnification of the eyepiece so that any further drift will be noticeable.

It is worth a reminder here not to spend too much time on polar alignment if you are observing visually, otherwise you will waste valuable observing time. However, if you are engaged in astronomical photography then you will need an accurate polar alignment, and the more accurate this is, the less work your guiding system will have to do to keep the telescope pointing in the right direction. Thankfully, with modern imaging techniques it is more usual these days to take a number of shorter exposures and then combine them in a computer, rather than the older techniques of taking pictures with exposures lasting many hours. In those days it was critical to have accurate polar alignment, but fortunately this is now not so much the case.

Aligning telescope optics

It's crucial to the quality of the view seen through a telescope to have the optics inside accurately aligned. It may be that the stars are not quite pinpricks of light or that planets are a little blurred, so checking up on the alignment is well worth the effort. A badly collimated first-class telescope is no better than a rubbish telescope. The process of aligning the optics is called *collimation* and is a task that with a little practice you will be performing with ease. Unfortunately, if you own a reflecting telescope then it is something that you will have to repeat quite regularly, particularly if you move the telescope around to different observing sites, because it is very easy to jolt them back out of alignment.

Collimation of a refractor is easier than collimation of a reflecting telescope so I shall cover that first. You will need to wait for a clear sky as this is a night-time activity in which you will ideally point your telescope at Polaris, the Pole Star. I have picked this object because, of all the stars in the sky, it does not move significantly over the period of time that you will be collimating your telescope. If your telescope has a right-angled eyepiece holder, known as a 'diagonal', then it needs to be removed for this exercise. Using a low-power eyepiece, one with a higher number printed on it, centre Polaris and then replace the eyepiece with a higher-power one (with a lower number), making sure Polaris is still centred.

Now adjust the focus of Polaris so it is a big blurred disk instead of a pinpoint star – you will see a bright dot surrounded by a series of concentric rings. If the collimation of your telescope is good, then the dot will be in the centre of the rings and you can carry on with your night's observing. However, a poorly collimated telescope will show the dot off-centre. Another pair of hands will help tremendously with the next steps. As you look through the telescope at the out-of-focus star image, get your helper to put their hand in front of the telescope tube but around the edge somewhere. You will see it silhouetted against the star and as they move their hand around, stop when it is nearest to the off-centred spot. While they keep their hand there, look at the front of the lens and you will generally see six screws: three with Phillips heads and three with Allen heads (tiny hexagonal shapes). Find the pair of screws nearest to your helper's hand, gently loosen by a small amount the Allen screw, and then gently tighten (but not too much) the Phillips screw.

Looking back through the eyepiece, the star will now be off-centre so move it back to the middle and examine the out-of-focus star image again. If you are lucky, you will now have a perfectly centred dot in the centre of the concentric rings. If you are a little less lucky, the dot will have now moved further towards the centre, or if you are very

▶ *An out-of-focus star image through a good-quality refractor will appear as a series of concentric rings, almost like the cross-section of an onion.*

unlucky it will have moved the wrong way and got worse. However, if it has improved, you just need to repeat the process and turn the same screws in the same direction a little more. But if it has got worse, you will need to adjust the other two sets of screws to bring the dot back towards the middle. Keep at it until the bright dot is in the centre and the rings are concentric, and your refracting telescope will be perfectly collimated.

Collimation of a reflecting telescope is a little more fiddly. Inside a typical reflecting telescope are two mirrors, the primary mirror and the secondary, and both are adjusted in the act of collimation. Rough collimation is simplest if you do it in daylight and you will find another pair of hands will help make the task much easier. So, to begin with, set the telescope up in daylight and look through the eyepiece holder without an eyepiece in place. You will see the secondary mirror directly in front of you and, using the adjustment screws on the mirror holder, which are accessed from the open end of the main tube, adjust the mirror so it appears central when you look through the eyepiece tube. You may find you need to adjust the bolts securing the mirror holder at the side of the tube to achieve this.

▲ *The first step in aligning mirrors is to make sure the secondary mirror is in the right place.*

The next task is to look at the reflection in the secondary mirror and you will see a reflection of the main primary mirror. There are usually three screws on the back of the secondary mirror itself, which adjust its tilt. Looking through the eyepiece holder, adjust these screws until you can see all of the primary mirror, centred in the reflection of the secondary mirror.

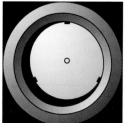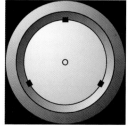

▲ *The angle of the secondary mirror is then adjusted so that the primary mirror is centred in the reflection.*

This next bit is where another pair of hands come in. Your willing helper needs to be down at the bottom end of the tube, behind the primary mirror. If you look at the way the mirror is mounted, you will see it is held in a mirror cell which has three (you may find more on larger mirrors but this is quite uncommon) adjustment screws or maybe wingnuts. These screws adjust the tilt of the primary mirror. Looking through the eyepiece holder again, focus your attention on the reflection in the primary

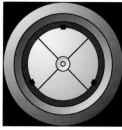

▲ *Finally, the primary mirror angle is adjusted so that the reflection of the secondary is in its centre.*

Aligning telescope optics

Traditional reflecting telescopes consist of
two mirrors which must be aligned with
each other and the eyepiece holder for a
good-quality image. Aligning them ensures
that none of the incoming light is wasted
or unnecessarily obstructed.

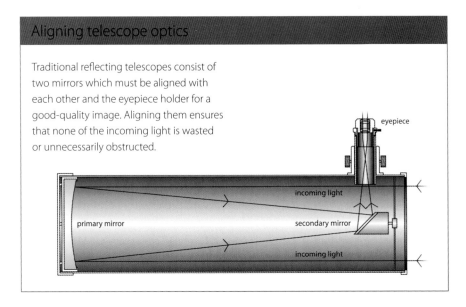

mirror and in it you will see another reflection of the secondary mirror (often a primary mirror
will have a tiny dot painted in its centre to help alignment). If the telescope is collimated
well, the secondary-mirror reflection will be in the centre of the primary mirror so you
can skip this next bit. But if the secondary-mirror reflection seems off-centre, then ask
your helper to gently turn one of the adjustment screws and watch to see if it brings the
mirror back towards the centre. If it makes it worse, then stop and turn it back the other
way. This step involves a little trial and error until you get the secondary-mirror reflection
in the centre of the primary mirror. Now you have completed this step, have a closer look at
the reflection of the secondary mirror – you will just about be able to see your eye looking
back at yourself!

At this stage, your reflecting telescope is only roughly collimated. To be sure you are
getting the best out of your telescope, you can fine-tune the collimation by taking it outside
at night when the sky is nice and steady and the stars are not twinkling too much. Point your
telescope at a reasonably bright star – Polaris is great because it does not move significantly
while you are collimating. Centre Polaris in the main telescope with a low-power eyepiece,
then change the eyepiece to a higher power and see if it is a nice crisp pinpoint. If it is not,
then you may need to tweak the collimation a little more.

While pointing at Polaris, adjust the focus a little so you are looking at a fuzzy view of it.
You will see a series of concentric rings with a dark dot in the middle, which is the shadow
of the secondary mirror. If the collimation is good, the dark spot will be in the centre of
the concentric rings, but if the spot is off-centre then more work is needed and you will
need to adjust the screws on the back of the primary mirror cell again, so that the circles
are concentric and the spot is moved back to the centre. Each time you adjust the screws
on the back of the mirror cell, recentre the star in the field of view before making more
adjustments.

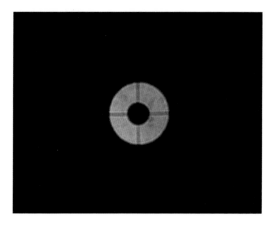

◄ *An out-of-focus star image through a collimated reflector shows the shadow of the secondary mirror perfectly centred.*

After you have collimated your telescope, be it refractor or reflector, you should see a noticeable improvement in the images you can see. On the other hand, if there are still problems and stars are not pinpoints or the out-of-focus star image is not circular, then you have other optical problems – perhaps the mirror or lens is too tightly held in its cell. Either way, go back to the supplier for help or pop along to your local astronomical society where you are likely to find someone who can help you further.

Finding objects

There are a number of steps to go through in order to be able to find things in the sky and I can teach you these, but you will need to stick with it and practise as much as possible, as there is only so far that I can take you – your own experience will take you the rest of the way. So you should now have your telescope set up, finder telescope aligned, optics all collimated, and telescope polar aligned if it is equatorially mounted. Now to the exciting bit of finding some celestial wonders!

The first step is to decide what you actually want to look at. That might seem like a crazy statement, but it is no good heading out with no plan of what you are hoping to see or you will waste loads of time. Consult Chapter 2 of this book to see what constellations are visible in the sky at the time you intend to observe. Having identified those, dig a little deeper and identify what objects are visible within those constellations. Once you have identified the items, order them so you start looking at objects setting over in the west and head eastwards slowly across the sky. Now you have planned your observing session, the next step is to actually find them!

Using the star charts, work out roughly where they should appear in the sky – for example, due north, south-east or west – and turn to face that direction. Orientate the star chart so it resembles the portion of the sky and identify some of the brighter stars near the object. For the brighter objects you can use the constellation charts in Chapter 2 to home in on your quarry, even if you are using binoculars, but for objects that are a little fainter, you will need something a little more precise so will need to get hold of star maps that show fainter stars and objects.

Earlier in the book we looked at the star-hopping technique to find objects, which works really well for locating the position of an object with the naked eye, and there is a pretty simple trick I find really useful when trying then to find the object through binoculars.

Once you have identified the location of the object (you may either have spotted it directly or at least found its location), then do not shift your gaze from that point and just raise your binoculars up to your eyes, making sure you do not move your gaze. You will be amazed that, more often than not, the object will be there, in the field of view of the binoculars. If you are looking for a fainter deep-sky object, then slowly make tiny movements of the binoculars to move the stars around and if you had not spotted your target before, it may well now pop into view. Once you know where it is in the field of view, you can always use averted vision to try and improve its visibility.

Finding things with telescopes can prove a little more difficult, although star hopping works really well because you can leave the telescope pointing at the object while quickly referring to a star chart, before looking back at the object again. Be warned, though – some telescopes invert the image, making everything seem to be back to front and upside down, which makes star hopping a little more tricky! It is worth sticking with it, though, as star hopping is a great skill to have and one that will never fail to work.

There are other options to finding things with a telescope. Some equatorial telescope mounts come equipped with setting circles, which are simply graduated scales fitted around the two axes of the telescope. The two scales represent the co-ordinates of right ascension and declination, and using them is almost like dialling up the co-ordinates of the object you are trying to find. It is not impossible to use a similar system on an altazimuth mount, but it is a lot more difficult and requires nearly constant adjustment. If you think back to Chapter 1 when we looked at co-ordinates and how the sky moves, then you will remember that declination is the celestial equivalent of latitude and the line representing the celestial equator, or 0° declination, will always be in the same place from your observing location, whatever time of year it is and whatever time of day. Once the telescope and the declination setting circle are set up, you will not need to fiddle with this any more, unless they get knocked. It may actually be that your telescope's declination setting circle is fixed and cannot be adjusted at all. Right ascension, on the other hand, moves as the Earth rotates so you might start observing with the line of right ascension representing 15 hours over in the east, but as the night progresses it moves through south to the west. Unlike declination, the right ascension setting circle will constantly need adjusting throughout the night. This might all sound a little fiddly, but it is actually quite simple.

Once your telescope is set up and roughly polar aligned, you then need to locate an easy-to-find object – a bright star will do and ideally one that is reasonably close to the object you are looking for. Look up its right ascension and declination, and once you have located it and, crucially, centred it in the field of view of a low- to medium-power eyepiece, you then need to check the declination circle is reading correctly and adjust the right ascension circle to read its right ascension. This is usually achieved by simply turning the circle until it reads the correct value. Now all you need to do is look up the value for the right ascension and declination of the object you are looking for, turn the mount so the two values read correctly on the setting circles and, hey presto, the object should be in the centre of the eyepiece!

The ultimate solution to finding objects in a telescope is to use one of the many computerized Go To telescope systems. These act like computerized setting circles and come in one of two different varieties. The cheaper version has a digital readout and gives guidance

◀ *Setting circles on telescope mounts help you to locate objects using their co-ordinates.*

on which direction to move the telescope, whereas the more expensive and now more common alternative will activate the motors to turn the telescope to point directly at the object you selected. In both cases, there is a simple alignment process involved at the start of an observing run which usually involves setting the date and time, the latitude and longitude of the observing location, and then pointing the telescope at one or two chosen stars that are selected off a list. From this, the telescope knows exactly where it is and where it is pointing, and by choosing the object you wish to observe from a list either guidance is given to move the telescope or it points at it for you. I started off trying to find things by star hopping and then, once I had a telescope equipped with them, I began using setting circles. Finally, with the availability of off-the-shelf electronics, I am now a big fan of using the Go To type of telescope, which takes all the hard work out of finding objects. Instead of taking time to find things, I can now use the time to observe them. With that said, I do still occasionally use other telescopes without any pointing aids so do keep my hand in with star hopping for many of the brighter objects. It is a skill that, once learned, never leaves you.

Cleaning mirrors and lenses

The first question you should ask yourself is, 'Do I really need to clean them?' The reason for asking yourself this question is simple: too many people clean telescope optics far too regularly. A small amount of contamination or dust on the lens or mirror will make no noticeable difference to the quality of the image – in fact, you would be surprised how much rubbish can be found on them before any image degradation is seen.

If you do decide it is the right time to clean, then make sure you mark the orientation of the mirror or lens in its holder before you remove it. This will allow you to put it back in the same position, but it is much more important with a lens than it is with a mirror. Once you have removed them, you must take great caution when handling and cleaning them. Be very careful not to touch the surfaces with your fingers – hold them around the edge so you do not get any grease on them. The first thing to do is to use compressed gas to try and dislodge any bits of dust or grit on the surface. Be careful not to let any of the propellant liquid from inside the can get on to the optics, so do not shake it before use. It is also worth releasing a squirt of air away from the optics before starting.

The next steps depend on whether you are cleaning a mirror or a lens. For mirrors, submerse them in a bowl of distilled water and, using cotton-wool balls, very gently wipe around the optics in a circular fashion while underwater, using the smallest amount of pres-

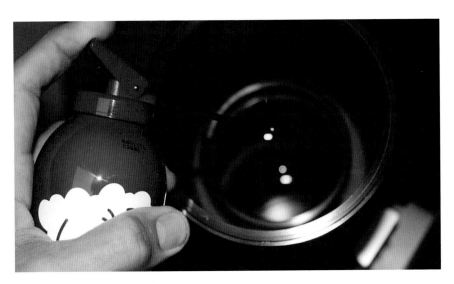

▲ *Great care must be taken when cleaning telescope optics. Canned air is a good way to clean off contaminants before making contact to clean off more stubborn marks.*

sure. Keep a swirling motion going in the water to prevent the rubbish from settling back on the optics again. It is crucial not to apply any real pressure as you could easily scratch the reflective surface – you just need to let the weight of the cotton-wool ball provide the pressure. Now remove the optics from the bowl, slipping it out edge-first which will keep contaminants from getting back on to the glass. If there are any stubborn marks, mix up a solution of 50% distilled water and 50% isopropyl alcohol (which is available from your local chemist) and soak a cotton bud so you can apply a little pressure just where it is needed to tease away the offending muck. Only use as much pressure as needed and only where needed.

Let the mirror dry by standing it on its side. You shouldn't get any drying marks as the water is distilled, but the last task will ensure the mirror is given a final clean. First make sure there are no pieces of stubborn muck or grit that you can see still sitting on the surface. Once it is totally free from contamination, take some isopropyl alcohol and pour a small amount in the centre. Using a very soft clean towel, buff the surface until all the alcohol has evaporated, but make sure you buff using a circular motion and only a little pressure.

If it is a lens you are cleaning, do not submerge it in a bowl of water because good-quality lenses are made up of more than one lens all fixed together. Submerging this lot in water could easily allow water to seep in between the elements, which will require professional assistance to resolve. A better method for cleaning telescope lenses is to make up a solution of 50% distilled water and 50% isopropyl alcohol, soak a cotton-wool ball in the liquid, and then drag it around the surface of the lens in a circular fashion, letting the weight of the ball provide the pressure. Any stubborn marks should be tackled with care and only enough pressure used to remove the offending dirt.

And that's it – you should now have an ultra-clean set of optics. All that remains is to put them carefully back in the telescope, align them, and you are back up and running.

chapter 5

ASTRONOMICAL ACCESSORIES

ASTRONOMY is one of those activities where gadgets are available by the truckload. Buying a telescope can be just the start, and with ranges of eyepieces, filters, cameras, finderscopes and all manner of other things, the real challenge is differentiating between which ones you 'need' and which ones you are seduced by and simply 'want' because they are just plain cool! Looking through my own collection I have got a fine selection of both, but I will contain my focus to those that I find most useful and warn you about some which are just a waste of money. You will find that some of my recommendations are for the keen amateur astronomer while others are for the beginner, so there is something for all.

One of the most essential accessories for any astronomer and one you should get hold of straight away is a **red torch**. We looked at dark adaptation and red torches in Chapter 1, but there is a wide range on the market. I have tried a lot of different ones over the years and have settled on two that work well for me. I now use a red torch that sits on my head, keeping my hands free to operate equipment, and a credit-card-sized torch which I can keep in my back pocket. The head torch was originally a white-light torch, so I painted the lens with a few thick layers of red translucent paint to make sure it was not too bright. You will remember from Chapter 1 that a bright red light can be as damaging as a white torch. It is also worth steering away from the red torches that allow you to switch to white light. These can easily and inadvertently be switched across when out in the field, ruining your dark adaptation as well as that of others. Bright red bicycle lights can be as damaging as they, like some red LED torches, can still be too bright. Make sure you keep a ready supply of spare batteries too, so you never find yourself in the dark.

Some form of **basic sky guide** is essential also, and this can come in a couple of different formats. Of course, this book will guide you around the sky throughout the year, but you may want something a little more detailed. A technological solution comes from the smartphones and tablet PCs now readily available. Smartphones are particularly useful as they are small and easily fit in your pocket. Whether you

◀ *A red torch is an essential piece of kit to help you see in the dark yet maintain your dark adaptation, allowing you to continue enjoying the night sky.*

▶ *Smartphone apps make finding things with the naked eye much easier and are available for most popular models of phone.*

are using a phone or a tablet, they are both clever enough to know where they are on the Earth from information from GPS satellites. By knowing the date and time, they will show you what can be seen in the sky from your location – some of the more advanced ones even have compasses inside which allow them to work out which direction you are pointing the phone, so you can hold it up to the sky and it will show you what you can see in that direction. Do be cautious with the amount of light from the screen, though, as this can be a bit bright. Many of the apps you can download have a night-time mode which switches the display to shades of red on black and, in conjunction with turning the brightness down, will remove a lot of the glare. If I'm observing with other people, I make sure not to give off too much light by sticking some red translucent film over the front of it to keep the light levels down.

Smartphones are great but sometimes they cannot get a GPS fix or the batteries run out. When this happens you need a back-up option and, for me, a **planisphere** is the ideal accessory to enable me still to find my way around. These were discussed in Chapter 1 and Philip's produce them for a number of different locations around the world. If your phone gives up, then a red torch and a planisphere will mean you can keep observing.

Chapter 2 already looked at choosing telescopes and how they are useless without a good-quality mount, but they are equally useless without a good set of **eyepieces**. Essentially, a telescope collects and focuses incoming starlight, while an eyepiece takes the resultant image and magnifies it. Choosing which type of eyepiece to buy

◀ *A planisphere is another great tool for learning your way around the sky, but do not forget to have your red torch handy to read it in the dark!*

▶ *A good selection of eyepieces are needed to give you a range of magnifications – remember, the number printed on them is their focal length.*

from the six or so popular designs can be bewildering, but there are a couple of things to consider that will help. If you have already searched out eyepieces then you will know that you can spend anything from £30 to £300, and in some cases even more. If you pay for cheap eyepieces then you will get lower-quality optics, and if you get lesser quality then the image will suffer. But, that said, 'fast' telescopes (telescopes with a low f/ratio such as f/4 or f/5) tend to be less forgiving and you should aim for higher-quality eyepieces, whereas 'slower' telescopes (with a high f/ratio around f/8 or f/9) can cope with lower-quality eyepieces and still yield a good sharp image. When choosing which eyepiece to go for, it is also worth thinking about the focal length of the eyepiece as, in my opinion, shorter-focal-length eyepieces tend to be less forgiving of poor quality than longer-focal-length eyepieces.

Quality is a little subjective as what is acceptable to one person may not be to another, but one of the more important and objective considerations when choosing eyepieces is the focal length. Eyepieces are almost like mini telescopes that collect light from the main telescope and magnify it, and it is this magnification which determines how 'big' the object appears through the eyepiece. Like telescopes, too, eyepieces have a focal length and this determines the magnification that you will get. It is important to note, though, how this will apply to your particular telescope. Put the same eyepiece in a telescope with a different focal length and you will get a different magnification. Working out the magnification that a telescope and eyepiece combination will give is a simple calculation: divide the focal length of the telescope by the focal length of the eyepiece. For example, a telescope with a 1,000 mm focal length and a 15 mm eyepiece will give a magnification of 66×, so you will see an image 66× bigger than you would see with the naked eye. You can use the calculation above in reverse to work out which eyepiece you need for a particular magnification. Simply divide the telescope focal length by the magnification you are after and that will tell you the focal-length eyepiece you need. Generally, an eyepiece with a big number (longer focal length) means a smaller image and an eyepiece with a smaller number (shorter focal length) means a bigger image!

Most telescopes come with one or two eyepieces, but as you observe you will realize that more than one eyepiece is needed to give you a range of magnifications to suit different objects and different conditions. You will get much more use out of the middle range of magnifications so concentrate on getting these first, perhaps a 24 mm and 12 mm eyepiece. You can then look to purchase a lower and higher focal length at a later date. Ultra-stable atmospheric conditions, which are essential to be able to use high-power eyepieces, are few and far between so there is no rush to get one of these – you might use it for just a few nights of the year, whereas lower-power eyepieces are much more forgiving of the conditions and so get used much more. My eyepiece collection consists of eyepieces of various brands with a good spread of focal lengths at 56 mm (53✕), 24 mm (125✕), 12 mm (250✕) and 6.4 mm (469✕), but of course on a different telescope you would get different magnifications. When choosing eyepieces, you must also bear in mind that the maximum useful magnification of your telescope is determined by around 20✕ magnification for every centimetre of aperture, so a 15 cm telescope could usefully manage a magnification up to around 300✕.

You will also hear eyepieces being described in terms of their field of view. There are actually two terms here: apparent field of view and true field of view. The apparent field of view is the amount of sky that can be 'seen' if you look through the eyepiece alone and is measured in degrees. This is not much practical use in itself, but using this figure along with the magnification of your eyepiece/telescope combination allows you to work out the true field of view. This is the actual portion of sky you will see when looking through your telescope and to calculate it you divide the apparent field by the magnification. For example, if you have an eyepiece with an apparent field of 50° and a magnification of 100✕, then you will get a true field of view of 0.5°, which is just about the size of the full Moon in the sky.

Another consideration with eyepieces is the distance between the eyepiece (or more accurately the outer surface of the lens) and your eye, known as 'eye relief' (see page 77). An eyepiece that has a small eye relief means you need to get your eye really close to the eyepiece to see the whole image, too far away and you will not be able to see it all. A longer eye relief is much more comfortable, but this can take a little practice to get your eye in just the right place to get the full image. Over the years I have tried many different eyepieces, some with such a low eye relief that I really had to squash my eye up to the eyepiece to see the image properly. It is not just about seeing the whole field of view but is about comfort too, and of particular interest to you if you wear glasses to observe. I am often asked if people should take their glasses off to observe, but it is

Eyepieces

Eyepieces can be thought of like a magnifying glass. The telescope lens or mirror brings incoming starlight to a focus and the eyepiece magnifies it.

Changing the eyepiece will change the magnification and the size of the resultant image.

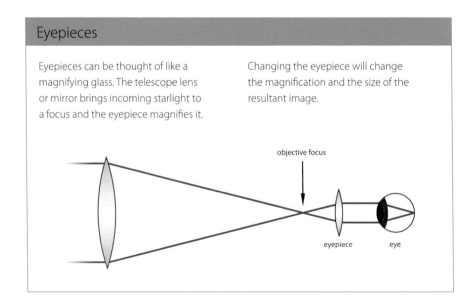

objective focus

eyepiece   eye

dependent on the condition. Short- or long-sighted people are normally fine as they can adjust the focus of the telescope to correct, but if you have astigmatism then you will need to keep glasses on or contact lenses in. If you do need to wear glasses, then try and get eyepieces with a long eye relief of about 20 mm or more.

You may also hear about the exit pupil of an eyepiece, which is the diameter of the beam of light coming out of the eyepiece. I am afraid this is also something you need to work out based on your telescope but it is very easy – just divide the eyepiece focal length by the telescope focal ratio. With my set-up, the 12 mm eyepiece on the telescope operating at f/11 gives me an exit pupil of 1 mm. The relevance here for the astronomer is that the brightness of extended objects like galaxies and nebulae decreases as the exit pupil decreases. Stars or planets, on the other hand, tend to retain their brightness with different sized exit pupils, getting dimmer only when viewed through telescopes with a smaller aperture. This is why the sky tends to get darker with higher magnification, because the exit pupil changes and the sky, which is effectively the largest of all extended objects, gets dimmer. You can use this to your advantage if you are observing in light-polluted skies as an exit pupil between 3 mm to 4 mm will start to darken the sky. If you are looking at planets it is best to aim for an exit pupil of between 1 mm to 2 mm, but a larger exit pupil is preferable for all extended objects.

A great accessory to your range of eyepieces is a **Barlow lens**. These fit between the eyepiece and telescope and act to either double or triple the magnification of an eyepiece. For example, a 20 mm eyepiece will, when used with a Barlow lens, perform like a 10 mm eyepiece, at least as far as magnification is concerned. Purchasing one good-quality Barlow lens and sensible eyepiece choices will mean you only have to buy half the number of eyepieces.

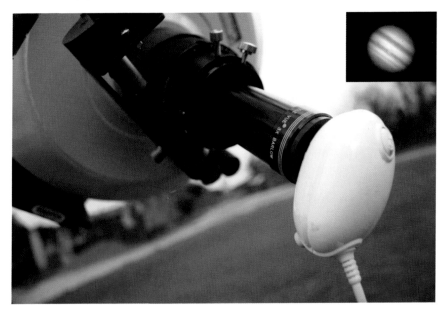

▲ *A Barlow lens multiplies the power of the view through the telescope, in this case the object is Jupiter, and can be used with eyepieces or a webcam.*

◀ *Illuminated reticule eyepieces superimpose illuminated markings on the view through a telescope, such as crosshairs.*

Barlow lenses can also be great for imaging applications because in most cases a camera will operate through a telescope without an eyepiece, so Barlow lenses can effectively double the focal length of the telescope and thus double the size of the image the camera can capture.

There are other types of eyepiece out there, such as those with illuminated reticules inside. These have either fine wires inside the lens or lines etched on to the glass that are illuminated by a faint red light. Through the eyepiece you will be able to see a gently glowing red cross or, in other designs, angular measurement scales – these are of great use in astronomical imaging and other more advanced applications. Whatever types of eyepiece you buy, make sure they fit in your telescope. Most beginners' instruments use 1.25" (31.7 mm) eyepieces, but 2" (50 mm) eyepieces are common amongst more advanced amateurs.

If you are the owner of a reflecting telescope, then a **collimation tool** is a worthy investment. Other types of telescopes like refractors are less susceptible to movement of the optics, whereas the collimation of the optics in a reflector needs regular attention. As you saw in Chapter 4, great collimation is achievable using stars, but a much quicker result can be gained by using a specially designed collimation tool. My favourites are the laser collimators, which work by fitting into the eyepiece holder and firing a laser beam at the secondary mirror. The principle is simple – the beam bounces down the tube and on to the primary mirror where it should strike the middle if the secondary is aligned correctly. It should then bounce back up the tube to hit the secondary again in the centre and back into the laser collimator if the primary is accurately aligned. They are easy to use and can be done in daylight too, without wasting valuable observing time.

You may find yourself a little disappointed with the view through a telescope, particularly when you start hunting down deep-sky objects, but it is possible to significantly enhance what you can see through the use of **filters**. More commonly, these are screwed into the telescope end of the eyepiece, but there are also variations and different sizes which can be fitted to cameras to enhance the images you are capturing. For visual

▶ *Laser collimators make the act of collimation much simpler by bouncing a laser beam off the mirrors of a reflecting telescope.*

◄ *Eyepiece filters help to enhance the view through a telescope. Check out the guide below to help you choose which filter is best for which object.*

observing, it is worth investing in a set of colour filters if you are interested in looking at the planets. The filters act to enhance the image as a result of the atmospheric scattering of light and in some cases to increase the contrast between different colours. They can be purchased in sets but make sure you get a set to fit the eyepiece size of your telescope – in most cases these will be

Filters for lunar and planetary observing

The **Moon** is a bright object and glare is one of the main reasons why surface detail cannot be seen. A green (#57) filter and a neutral density filter will cut down the glare, giving the surface detail much more contrast.

Mercury is only ever visible low in the twilight sky so light scatter is the main cause of poor image quality. A red (#25) or orange (#21) filter will help to enhance the surface detail by reducing the scattering of light.

Venus is easier to observe than Mercury, but the entire planet is covered in cloud so the only details visible are the subtle clouds high in its atmosphere, and for this a deep blue (#46) filter will enhance things nicely.

There is much more to see on **Mars** and most filters enhance some feature or other. I find the red (#25) filter the best at enhancing surface detail and defining the edges of the polar caps, but magenta (#30) also helps to enhance their detail. Blue (#80A) filters are good at helping to detect clouds in the Martian atmosphere.

The detail in the atmosphere of **Jupiter** can be greatly enhanced by the use of filters. Blue filters work best to improve the contrast of the Great Red Spot so something like the medium blue (#80A) would be a good start. Other features in the equatorial belts can be enhanced with a red (#25) filter, while polar region details really stand out with a yellow (#12) filter.

Saturn has features similar to Jupiter which can be seen by studying the upper layers of gas that the planet is made from. Red (#80A) and yellow (#12) will enhance the belts on the planet and a light green (#57) really brings out details in the rings.

Both **Uranus** and **Neptune** are much harder to observe than the rest due to their great distances from us. They appear blue in colour and brighten considerably in telescopes above 25 cm aperture, but green (#57) filters help to bring out the subtle details; however, do not expect too much from them.

1.25″ (31.7 mm) filters. Many of the sets of filters for planetary observing come as a set of four with varying choices of colours, and the set you choose will be determined by the objects and details you wish to observe.

It is always worth experimenting with filters to try and get the best result, as you may find a darker or lighter version of the same colour gives better results for you. The numbers quoted in the panel opposite refer to the filter's Wratten reference number – although the number does not follow any particular system, the accompanying letters refer to increasing colour density, so a light green filter is #57 whereas a darker version would be numbered #57D.

It is not just the planets that benefit from filtration at the eyepiece, as deep-sky objects can also be improved. So-called 'light-pollution filters' are a little bit misleading, though, because although they do cut down on light pollution, they also cut down on the light given off from stars and galaxies – as a result, not only does the sky darken but so do the objects themselves. However, they do work quite well on nebulosity and enhance the view, making the nebula a little more visible, so should perhaps be considered nebula filters rather than light-pollution filters.

There are other types of filters which are classed generically as narrow-band filters. As the name suggests, a narrow-band filter only allows light through from a very specific and narrow part of the spectrum, making the objects pop into view. The most popular are UHC (Ultra High Contrast), O III (pronounced 'oh-three') and H-beta filters. Like the light-pollution filters, a narrow-band UHC filter also cuts down the light pollution but enhances nebulosity much more, so I would certainly purchase a UHC filter in preference to a light-pollution filter. The O III filter is by far the best for enhancing planetary nebulae but I find that the UHC is better for emission nebulae. The H-beta only has limited use but is excellent for helping to detect certain emission nebulae like the Horsehead Nebula in Orion. As far as which one to buy, I would definitely recommend the UHC filter as a great all-round nebula filter; only after you have one of these would I consider getting an O III filter, and the H-beta only if you have spare cash or are keen to see the Horsehead.

A section about filters is not complete without discussion of **solar filters**. A number of cheap telescopes on the market come equipped with solar filters that fit over the eyepiece end of the telescope. These are dangerous because all the light and energy from the Sun has already been focused and magnified and is very likely to crack the filter without any warning, allowing the energy from the Sun straight in your eye. The only safe option for solar observing is either to project the image from the telescope on to a piece of white card or to buy filters which fit over the front end of the telescope and cut down

▶ *Projecting an image of the Sun is a cheap and safe way to study our nearest star.*

▲ *Red-dot finders project a red dot on the sky to help locate objects through telescopes.*

the energy before it enters the optical system. These can either be visual light filters or H-alpha filters, which are much more expensive but reveal stunning solar detail.

I do not think I have ever seen a telescope which does not come with a **finder telescope** of some sort. Chapters 3 and 4 covered these, but it is worth investing in a decent one if your telescope comes with one which is under par. It is essential to get a nice bright image through a finder to enable you to see plenty of stars and help you find your way around the sky. To be useful an optical finder needs to have an aperture of at least 30 mm, and for comfort it should include a diagonal, which sends its eyepiece out at a right angle to the tube of the finder telescope. Many people are starting to use red-dot finder telescopes, which project a tiny red light on to a glass screen on an unmagnified view of the night sky. These are great for lining up if you know exactly where an object is, but if you need to star hop then an optical finder is unrivalled. A great solution is to have both red-dot finder and optical finder so you are covered for all eventualities.

One type of finder worth steering clear of is the **laser pointer finder**! These are simply laser pointers attached to the side of the telescope and are aligned so the beam points in exactly the same direction as the telescope – by getting the laser beam pointing at the object, you will have the telescope pointing at it too. The lasers used for these must have a visible beam for them to work, but unfortunately this means that they are generally quite powerful, around 5 MW. It is all too easy to forget that you have a laser strapped to the telescope as you wield it around the sky and this puts pilots of aircraft and bystanders at risk of getting a laser beam in their eye. The reference to pilots may seem a little unexpected, but even a 5 MW laser can be enough to illuminate a cockpit and distract a pilot with potentially disastrous consequences. Already in the United States someone has been convicted with a

▶ *Star diagonals adjust the position of the eyepiece to make a more comfortable viewing angle.*

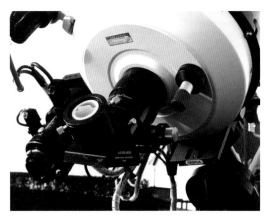

custodial sentence through the misuse of lasers and endangering an aircraft in flight. In reality, a 5 MW laser is not strong enough to damage anyone's eyesight because the human reaction to blink is sufficiently fast that no damage would occur – *but* the issue lies with the quality of the testing, as many 5 MW lasers are more powerful than the stated 5 MW and these are the ones that can cause damage. Another use for lasers is in education to show people around the sky and I have used these successfully on TV shows. But I should stress we take great care to ensure that there are no aircraft in the area and that at no time will I point the laser low to the horizon if there are people in the vicinity. The conclusion here is that laser pointers should not, in my opinion, be used on telescopes as finder telescopes, but they can be a useful aid to education when used with care, considering aircraft and bystanders at all times.

Star diagonals are a great addition to your kit bag, particularly if you own a refracting or catadioptic telescope. Pointing these telescopes low near the horizon is fine as the eyepiece is easily accessible and positioned for comfortable viewing, but if you point higher in the sky, perhaps up near the zenith, then you will find it really uncomfortable to view and almost

▲ *Two eyes are better than one! Bino-viewers let your brain see the same image twice, making it seem much clearer.*

impossible with some telescopes. A star diagonal turns the eyepiece through 90° and sends it out to the side, so it becomes much more comfortable to view when pointing at high altitudes. Be sure to get one of good quality though, otherwise you could be compromising an otherwise excellent optical system.

Another optical accessory I have tried but have mixed feelings about is the **bino-viewer** attachment, which allow you to use two eyes through a telescope rather than one. The concept is simple: if you can see something with two eyes, then the brain 'believes' it more and the image somehow becomes more prominent! It is a crazy idea but then the brain works in bizarre ways. I have used one to look at the Sun (with appropriate – and expensive – filters) and the planets and it takes quite a bit of getting used to, but the resultant image does seem brighter and crisper. One downside is that you have to buy two sets of eyepieces and these should ideally be a matched pair, sharing identical optical properties, so it does get a little more expensive.

With the exception of cloud, one of the biggest environmental challenges facing the astronomer is dew. Placing a large lump of glass outside at night, even if it is mounted in a protective telescope tube, with the cold night air swirling around it is asking for trouble. The cooler air causes the formation of dew not only on the optics but also often over the whole telescope. Dew on the telescope itself is not really a problem as long as it is left to dry out properly before packing away, but dew on the optics will render the telescope useless so a little investment in dew-busting gadgets is essential. Reflecting telescopes are

less susceptible to dew because the mirror is buried at the end of a long tube, but they can still be affected if the conditions are right. On the other hand, refracting or catadioptic telescopes, which have lenses at the front end of the telescope, can be badly affected because they are much more exposed to the elements. A good and simple solution is to buy or build a **dew shield**, which is just a plastic or metal extension to the telescope tube. I have seen perfectly good ones made out of lengths of vinyl floor covering and gaffer tape! For smaller telescopes they only need to stick out the front of the tube by no more than 30 cm, though further for larger instruments. Alternatively, you can buy them ready-made off the shelf for your specific telescope.

◀ *Dew shields help to delay the development of dew on telescope optics, particularly those with a lens.*

◀ Dew straps keep the temperature of telescope optics just above the temperature for dew to form.

A more expensive solution is to use **electric dew zappers**. These are strips of special electrical 'tape' which heat up gently when electricity is passed through them. Many of them require a controller of some sort, which will allow you to vary the amount of current passing through them to control how much they heat up. Some are even computer controlled, but by warming the strip of material which is wrapped around the tube where the lens is fitted will keep it just warm enough to stop the formation of dew. Often one controller will control more than one dew strap, so if you have a telescope and a guide telescope then you can control them all from one box – you can even get heaters for eyepieces to stop them dewing up. Ultimately, though, there will be times when the dew gets the better of your optics and when that happens you have two choices: try and get rid of the dew or pack up and go to bed. If you want to get rid of the dew, one of the best methods is to use a **hair dryer** on a gentle heat setting and gently blow warm air across the surface of the optics to slowly disperse the dew. You can get 12-volt camping hair dryers to run off battery power supplies and these are great when working out in the field. Whatever you do, under no circumstances should you take a cloth and wipe dew off the optics, because you risk scratching the glass.

Not only do you need to protect the telescope and equipment from the cold night environment, but you also need to make sure you are dressed appropriately. I covered this quite a bit in Chapter 1, but a great little gadget which I could not do without is an **electric hand warmer**. I actually have two, one for each hand as keeping them warm is half the battle in making your whole body feel warm. They can even charge up from USB leads, which is great if you do not have mains power but you do have a laptop.

Choosing suitable **cameras** for capturing astronomical images is itself a bit of a huge topic and I cover this a lot more in *Philip's Astrophotography with Mark Thompson*. There is more about this in the next chapter too, but the camera you choose will to a degree depend on the objects you wish to take pictures of. If you are interested in images of the Milky Way, constellations or meteor showers, then a DSLR camera will be needed. It is

▶ USB hand warmers are great for keeping your hands warm on cold nights.

◀ *DSLR cameras are great for newcomers to start astronomical imaging.*

important to get good-quality lenses to capture nice pinpoint star images and I prefer fixed-focal-length lenses rather than the multitude of zoom lenses on the market as the results are always a little better. You can always then attach a DSLR to a telescope to capture beautiful colour images of the night sky; however, to get the best out of them you need to get them modified. Most DSLRs have chips inside them that are sensitive to infrared radiation and if left alone they would produce pictures with a slightly odd colour balance. To resolve this, manufacturers install filters to remove the majority of the infrared radiation. This is no good for astronomy, though, because the filters also remove a lot of the light in the wavelength necessary to capture emission nebulosity, so to get the best out of them, the filters need to be removed or replaced with something a little more transparent.

If you are looking at capturing planetary pictures then you cannot beat the results from a webcam and telescope, and you will find that any of those on the market will produce results of some sort. These too will need modifying before you can use them, by removing the lens of the webcam and replacing it with an adaptor which allows it to fit into the eyepiece holder of the telescope. I have seen people suggest taking an old-style 35 mm film canister and gluing it to the body of the webcam to get the same effect, but it is critical that the webcam chip sits at the right angle to the incoming light and this cannot be guaranteed through this approach.

▶ *Webcams attached to a telescope can capture stunning planetary images.*

▶ *CCD cameras are the ultimate astronomical imaging tool.*

Instead, spend a few pounds to buy one of the easily available adaptors and replace the lens with it – job done.

For capturing the best results of deep-sky objects, a CCD camera is needed. The camera you buy will need to be one where the size of pixels (which are the light-sensitive detectors) match the focal length of your telescope. In other words, you need to be able to achieve a resolution of no less than about 1 arc second per pixel. You also need to be sure you are getting a good field of view, which is based on the size of the whole CCD chip and, again, the focal length of the telescope. Another very useful feature of most CCD cameras is set-point cooling, which basically means you can specify the temperature at which you wish the CCD camera to operate. This enables you to lower the electronic noise of the detector and allow it to operate more efficiently.

You can get mono or colour CCD cameras, but you get so much more flexibility and resolution in a mono camera that it is the only choice in my opinion. Mono CCD cameras are full of individual light-sensitive pixels which detect and record light, and these all go to make up the image. As you will see in the next chapter, you can still get a colour picture by using colour filters, but with a one-shot colour camera you need red pixels, green pixels and blue pixels to make up one 'colour' pixel. This lowers the resolution of the chip by one-third of a mono camera. Using mono also allows you to delve into the world of narrow-band imaging, where you can get some fabulous shots of nebulosity by using specialist filters.

◀ *Driven camera mounts allow you to increase exposure times without producing star trails.*

▲ *The Bahtinov mask makes focusing your camera through a telescope a lot easier.*

Another great photographic accessory is the **driven camera mount**, which is a tiny equatorial mount specifically to mount cameras on. Their purpose is to allow you to take night-sky photographs with DSLR cameras and standard camera lenses without being subjected to limited exposure times because of the rotation of the Earth. They need to be polar aligned just like telescope mounts, but because of the shorter-focal-length lenses in use this does not need to be done very accurately. Usually a polar scope is included to facilitate this, but once aligned they will allow you to take either wide-field or tighter shots of stars without the stars trailing. I have seen some stunning shots of the Milky Way that have been taken with these set-ups and they are great too for trying to capture meteor showers.

If you are a keen astronomical photographer, you will know how difficult it can be to get your camera to a precise focus through a telescope. If you are not lucky enough to have a motorized focusing system with the software to do the whole job for you then help is at hand from a **Bahtinov mask**! The mask fits over the front end of the telescope and is composed of three areas with thin lines cut into it. The groups of lines point in three different directions and produce three angled diffraction spikes, so when you look at a bright star with the mask in place, it will have three lines cutting through it. As the focus is adjusted, the central spike will seem to move left and right between the other two spikes. Perfect focus is achieved when the central spike is in the centre of the other two spikes. This wonderfully simple design takes the guesswork out of focusing, making it a precise and accurate job every time.

With more and more accessories requiring power, it is getting more and more essential to get power out to your telescope system. Another ideal accessory is to get a **portable 12-volt power supply** – these come in conveniently mounted plastic boxes with handles, allowing you to power your telescope and equipment without having an annoying (and dangerous) trailing mains power lead out into the garden.

Of all the accessories there is one final one which I think is amongst the most essential, yet it is not something you would necessarily expect to find in an astronomer's kit bag. It is a decent set of **tools**! I have lost count of the times I have needed a screwdriver or an Allen key while out in the field for all manner of tasks, from changing batteries in torches to collimation tweaks and dangling wires snagging on the mount to cable repairs. The complexity of your set-up will determine the extent of your toolkit, but for a beginner I would still recommend a couple of screwdrivers, a set of Allen keys (be aware that these come in either metric or imperial sizes so make sure you get the right set), some gaffer tape (which always comes in useful to cover over bright lights or stick down wayward cables) and some spare batteries for any of your accessories. If your set-up has more kit then your toolkit should be stocked to deal with any repairs or adjustments. I even have a soldering iron, solder and electronic multimeter in my set-up so I can try and fix electrical problems, but this is probably a bit extreme!

Essential accessories

We have covered a lot of accessories in this chapter so I thought it might be useful to group them all into either 'essential to have', 'nice to have' or 'avoid these' lists:

Essential to have
- A set of eyepieces appropriate for your telescope
- Dew-zapping equipment (including a hair dryer)
- Red torch
- Basic sky guide (planisphere or smartphone)
- Additional/adequate finder telescope
- Star diagonal (particularly for telescopes with eyepiece 'at the back')

Nice to have
- Barlow lens
- Collimation tool
- Electric hand warmer
- 12-volt portable power supply
- Filters (planetary, lunar or solar, UHC and O III)
- Bino-viewer
- Laser pointer (but only if used sensibly)
- Camera (webcam, DSLR or CCD)
- Driven camera mount
- Bahtinov mask

Avoid these
- Laser pointer finders
- Light-pollution filters
- Cheap eyepiece-mounted solar filters

chapter 6
ADVANCED AMATEUR ASTRONOMY

A STRONOMY is one of those hobbies where you can get as involved as you like. Many people are happy to read books and magazines, others to watch television shows to enhance their knowledge, while many find the act of gazing upon a dark star-filled sky with just their eyes sufficient to quench their thirst for the Universe. There are some who spend their lives hunting down faint elusive galaxies or returning to the planets time and time again, never getting enough of the view of our neighbours in space. For a few others, there needs to be more to it and fortunately there really is something for everyone. Astronomy is one of the few sciences where amateurs can still actively get involved in real research and help the professional astronomers to further our understanding of the Universe. The reason is simple: the sky is a big place and there are only a small number of professional telescopes worldwide. The thousands of amateur astronomers around the world can help by turning their telescopes to the sky and provide information that would otherwise be lost.

There are astronomical projects which suit all areas of interest and all levels of experience so there is something you can find to keep you amused, from observing planetary atmospheres to hunting for exploding stars and searching for new comets. The great thing is, for the most part, none of them require anything more than a telescope and your eyes. Certainly, some of the projects will have a greater scope with more advanced equipment, but you can always develop your involvement as your equipment grows.

Planetary observations

One of the easiest projects for the beginner to get started on involves studying the planets for significant changes in appearance. Perhaps a dust storm has whipped up on Mars or a new storm has appeared on the gas giant Jupiter, and detecting and observing features like these are a great help to professional astronomers trying to understand them better. Many people think that with the advent of space exploration and robotic probes to the planets there is little the amateur can do to help, but in all cases the probes have a finite lifespan and can only observe for a limited period of time. An experienced amateur astronomer studying a planet can provide crucial supporting information. Indeed, some of Sir Patrick Moore's Moon drawings were used during the Apollo Moon landings.

The key to good planetary observations is firstly to wait for nights of good 'seeing' when the view through a telescope is nice and stable, revealing high levels of detail, and also to be diligent in making observations. Often this can be making drawings on templates

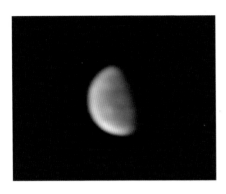

◀ *Mercury is hard to spot and only visible just before sunrise or just after sunset.*

provided by many of the pro–am organizations or taking images on computer, but at all times make notes of dates, times, conditions and the equipment you were using.

Mercury is perhaps the hardest planet to observe due to its proximity to the Sun in the sky. Even if it can be seen, it is very difficult to detect any surface detail because it is small and so far away from us. The competition is stiff too, since NASA's Messenger mission has almost completely mapped the surface details of the entire planet in high resolution, but things do change. However, for the amateur astronomer, trying to detect or image surface detail on the innermost planet is perhaps only of personal interest.

Venus, on the other hand, provides more opportunity for useful study even though the entire planet is covered in thick cloud. The surface remains hidden from view unless radar technology is used to pierce through the cloud and this has been done very successfully by the Magellan spacecraft. The interest for the amateur astronomer lies in studying the detail in the atmosphere and trying to pick out elusive features. This can be done visually or through imaging, but the use of filters can greatly enhance what you can see. As we saw in Chapter 5, a deep blue filter will enhance detail in the clouds, and drawings or images of the observed features are of use. If you are relying on drawing features then you must employ a lot of self control just to draw the features you can see, not those which you think you can see as these are of no scientific value. Information from the features in the clouds will enable

timings to be made of the rotation periods of the visible markings at different latitudes, and provide a better understanding of the winds in the atmosphere.

If you are kitted out with a camera, you can make infrared observations of the crescent Venus to reveal information about the planet's thermal emissions. One of the less well understood phenomena is called the 'ashen light', which is a faint and subtle glow of light coming from the night-time side of the planet. This is similar to the Earthshine seen on the dark portion of the Moon, which

▶ *The clouds of Venus (pictured here from NASA) can be nicely enhanced with a deep blue filter.*

glows gently because it is illuminated by reflected sunlight bouncing off the Earth. Any observations of that too can be of great use in trying to understand the underlying processes.

The red planet Mars is easier to identify in the sky but, because of its orbit, only appears well placed in our sky at opposition every two years. Even then, it is only a decent size for a couple of weeks either side of opposition, making opportunities for good-quality observations few and far between. When it is visible, observations are focused around three particular phenomena. Violent dust storms can whip up and sometimes engulf the entire planet, and these can be seen from Earth in amateur telescopes. If they last for a long time they can affect the climate. Careful study of the dark features on the Martian surface and identification of changes in their appearance reveal the movements of these dust storms. Filters can greatly enhance their visibility and contrast, particularly for visual work. The driving force for these winds is solar heating, just like the weather here on Earth.

Mars also experiences seasons like the Earth and its carbon dioxide polar caps can be seen to shrink and grow as the seasons change. Studying and recording these changes will help to understand how the seasons on Mars are slowly changing. Filters again can be used to search for white wisps of cloud in the Martian atmosphere. These help to build a better understanding of how the atmosphere of Mars is slowly changing and evolving over long periods of time. A telescope of at least 15 cm is needed to get the most out of studying Martian detail, but do not forget to use filters to enhance the view.

An easier target for the beginner with a modest telescope is Jupiter which, when visible, tends to present a decent-sized image in the eyepiece. Being a gas giant planet, observations reveal detail in the upper layers of its atmosphere and there is always lots going on. The first things you will notice when looking at Jupiter are the numerous belts which circle the planet. Usually the most prominent are the north and south equatorial belts, which run either side of the equator. Embedded in the southern belt is the famous Great Red Spot, which is a huge hurricane storm that has been raging for hundreds of years. It is also possible to see other belts of varying prominence, white spots which represent additional storms, and other disturbances among the belt systems. Try out a red or yellow filter to improve the belts and a blue filter on the Great Red Spot. Observations of storms and disturbances are usually recorded with a longitude reference on Jupiter to point other observers in the right direction for follow-up observations.

Like Jupiter, Saturn is also a large gas planet but with an incredible system of rings that are visible in most telescopes. Useful observations of the planet include recording details in the belts visible in the atmosphere

◀ *The polar caps of Mars are a good photographic target for beginners.*

▶ *Atmospheric detail of Jupiter, such as the Great Red Spot, is revealed in any good beginner's telescope. This image from NASA reveals the swirling violent nature of the storm.*

of Saturn. Occasionally brighter, quite obvious, features appear on Saturn and when they do it is useful to record the time when they 'transit' or pass the centre of the disk of the planet. If you are recording your observations by drawing what you can see, templates of the planet can be downloaded off the internet or acquired from many of the amateur astronomy organizations. Carefully recording the location of the shadow of the rings is also of use, as is noting down the relative intensity of the features and the different rings that can be seen. On rare occasions, Saturn will pass in front of (occult) a star and it is useful to record the brightness of the star and how and when it fades or brightens. Another more challenging pursuit, which requires imaging equipment, is to record the subtle brightness changes of the many moons of Saturn. Software is available which can do this much more accurately than just visual observations will allow.

▲ *The atmosphere of Saturn is less prominent than that of Jupiter, but the rings are great to study. This image from NASA shows how truly magnificent they are.*

Searching for comets and asteroids

▲ *Asteroids like Gaspra are easily within the reach of amateur astronomers, both photographically and visually, but they will only appear as a tiny spec of light, unlike this image which was captured by NASA.*

Not everything in the Solar System is reliable or indeed predictable since, on occasions, new comets or asteroids swing into view. Asteroids tend to be on moderately stable orbits but they are often small and dark and very difficult to detect, so there are still plenty of discoveries being made by amateur astronomers that are missed by the automated sky searches going on around the globe. There was once a time when astronomers would become so familiar with small patches of sky that they would look at it night after night and immediately spot something which had moved or suddenly appeared! This was a time-consuming approach to finding asteroids, but now with the advent of the CCD camera the job has become a whole lot easier.

To improve your chances of finding one, then the bigger the telescope you can use the better, as gathering as much light as possible is the key. Telescopes of at least 15 cm aperture should be used with an equatorial mount and drive system. Using the camera attached to the telescope, snap three or four images of the same area of sky over a period of a couple of hours. It is best to focus on areas of sky around the ecliptic as that is where the highest concentration of asteroids will be lurking. The images are then loaded into software, which is readily available on the internet, and the software will alternately display the images so that anything which is new or has moved will 'blink' as the image changes. This technique is called 'blink comparison' and is also used when searching for supernovae. Additional software will usually allow you to identify the object's position instantly, and a quick check online with the Minor Planet Center (MPC) in Massachusetts, USA, will tell you if you have found something new or something that is already known about. If it is new, you will need to capture another image on another night to confirm your sighting and then submit all the details online to the MPC. If all is well and it is confirmed, then you will be accredited with its discovery. This sounds easy in principle but it is worth starting out by making observations of known asteroids first to practise, and once you are getting reliable results, you can strike out looking for new objects.

Comet hunting, on the other hand, is a little more forgiving and can be done using visual methods rather than photographic. The appearance of comets is usually of a fuzzy blob of varying degrees of brightness depending on proximity and a number of other factors. Generally, for visual patrols, the brighter comet suspects are your potential quarry, so to improve your chances of finding a brighter comet you need to concentrate your search

▶ *Comets like Hyakutake are often discovered by amateur astronomers and can put on a stunning display. This photograph shows the comet next to Polaris, above the Hawaiian islands.*

on the western sky a few hours after sunset, and the eastern sky a few hours before dawn. Comets brighten as they approach the Sun, so the brighter ones will be found in this portion of the sky – start low in the west when you can see a reasonable number of stars and slowly sweep across the sky heading upwards until you get due south-west. Any comets lurking beyond this area are likely to be reasonably faint and worth leaving for the larger scopes or those hunters with imaging equipment.

The best telescope for this type of work is a relatively fast reflector – something at least 15 cm aperture and with a low f/ratio. A systematic sweep across the sky will eventually reveal fuzzy blobs, so cross-check the suspect with a star chart to see if it is a galaxy, nebula, cluster or even a known comet. If it is not, then check back on the object about 30 minutes later. If it is a comet it will eventually move, so if it is still stationary 30 minutes later, wait another 30 minutes. Once you are certain it has moved and so *must* be a comet, and once you have triple-checked all known comets in that area of sky, even those which are fainter than your telescope can detect just in case it has unexpectedly brightened, then you will need to note down your observation. This should include date, time, co-ordinates and appearance of the comet, along with an estimate of its apparent size in degrees or minutes of arc. With all of this information to hand, it needs to be reported to the Central Bureau for Astronomical Telegrams, and if it is confirmed and if no one else has beaten you to it, then the comet will be named after you. Congratulations!

Searching for supernovae

A similar approach to hunting for asteroids and comets is used when searching for super-novae and either visual or photographic techniques can be used. Supernovae are among the most violent explosions in the Universe, but the processes behind them vary. There are two types of supernova: Type I and Type II, both of which ultimately lead to the destruction of a star. Type Ia supernovae are the result of a binary star system usually composed of an ageing white dwarf star and a companion star. The mass of the white dwarf is sufficient to drag material off the companion star and on to itself. If the additional material leads to the white dwarf reaching a critical mass that is 1.38 times the mass of the Sun, then the star is unable to stop itself collapsing due to the weight of the extra material. The collapse causes an increase in temperature and pressure inside the star, leading to a significant amount of the stellar material undergoing cataclysmic nuclear fusion in just a few seconds, causing the star to explode as a supernova. A variation of this Type Ia event is where two white dwarf stars merge, although this does not always lead to a supernova explosion. All other supernova types, including the Type Ib, Type Ic and Type II, are the result of the collapse of the core of a supermassive star. The core collapse occurs for different mass stars at different stages, but ultimately the fusion in the core becomes unstable and it is unable to support itself against the immense force of gravity. The core collapses and causes the catastrophic expulsion of the

▲ *The tiny ring structure, above centre, is the remains of a star that went supernova.*

outer layers into space. Depending on the mass of the star, either a neutron star, pulsar or black hole will be the end result.

Searching for these exploding stars is a little bit like looking for the proverbial needle in a haystack with your eyes shut, so do not expect instant results. Unless you are very lucky you will need to look at or image thousands of galaxies, if not more, before capturing your first supernova. If you are employing visual searching techniques, then a good starting point would be to choose a selection of galaxies and limit your search to about 20, and get hold of some accurate star charts of that area of sky. These need to be pretty detailed and show stars to a level of brightness that is a couple of magnitudes below the threshold of your telescope. Then simply observe the galaxy and compare stars in the field of view, looking beyond the visible extent of the galaxy as you will not be able to detect its fainter outer regions and there may well be a supernova lurking there. See anything that does not appear on the chart? Then double-check for variable stars that might have brightened – asteroids are also worth checking, so look a few times over the next couple of hours to make sure it does not move. While you are doing all of this, get a friend to take a look too or get them to grab some images if they have an imaging set-up. If you are sure that you have eliminated all possible explanations and that it must be a new supernova, then notify the Central Bureau for Astronomical Telegrams with all the details.

The approach is a little different if you have an imaging set-up, because more galaxies can be studied, particularly if you have sufficient equipment that you can automate the whole task. That may sound like the stuff of professional astronomy, but all the necessary bits and bobs can be bought off the shelf so it is well within the scope of the amateur set-up. For the manual approach to a photographic search for supernovae, a selection of galaxies should be chosen and they should be imaged individually with an exposure of about 30 seconds. Compare the images with search charts to make sure there are no unexpected objects, and if they are clean you can use this as your reference image for the galaxy. The principle from here on is to take further images of the same galaxy, then align the new image with the old image in software that will allow you to flash the two images alternately so that new objects appear to blink in and out of view. This saves painstakingly checking each star in the image and can highlight potential candidates quickly and easily. There are other events which can catch you out when employing photographic techniques, such as cosmic-ray strikes on the detector, 'hot' pixels, noise and many more. But once you have identified a potential supernova and have ruled out all of the above, then the image with details can be sent over to the Central Bureau for Astronomical Telegrams who will confirm the discovery, or not. Time is of the essence, so if you are unable to complete follow-up observations ask a friend to help.

Monitoring variable stars

Many of the stars visible in the night sky are members of binary or multiple star systems and it is only their careful study which reveals their true nature. Along the same vein, careful study of starlight reveals that some of them are variable stars, which means the amount of light or energy they give off over a period of time varies. The types of variable stars can be grouped into three broad categories: *pulsating*, *eclipsing* and *eruptive*, and observing these is a popular project for amateur astronomers.

Pulsating variable stars, as their name suggests, are stars that shrink and grow, leading to a variation in the amount of light they emit. The period of time over which this variation takes place also varies – there are some pulsating variables which vary on an irregular basis, others on a semi-regular basis, while some are like clockwork, such as the Cepheid variable stars which are used as standard candles to measure distances in the Universe. This class of variable star has a link between period of variation and amount of light given off, so by measuring how long it takes for them to vary means their absolute or intrinsic brightness can be determined. From this it is possible make a comparison with their apparent brightness in the sky and then estimate their distance.

Eclipsing binary stars can actually be two or more stars in orbit, whose orbits lie along our line of sight. This means that, from our vantage point here on Earth, we see the stars alternately pass in front of each other and when they do we see the brightness of the system drop. If a graph is drawn with brightness plotted against time, then maximum brightness would be seen when both stars were completely visible, but it would show two drops in brightness as the stars eclipse each other. Algol, in Perseus, is a great example of an eclipsing binary system, taking just over 3 days to complete a full cycle. There are some eclipsing binary stars that can only be seen spectroscopically, which means their presence is only given away by studying the spectra and watching for the tell-tale signs. Unless you are serious about this kind of work, spectroscopic binaries are best left to professional astronomers.

The final type of variable star is the eruptive variable which, as its name suggests, is much more impressive, in nature if not in appearance. Eruptive variables tend to remain quite insignificant for most of the time but suddenly, and often unexpectedly, brighten by a few magnitudes before fading away again. Novae are great examples of this, which are usually binary stars where material like hydrogen gets sucked from one star on to the other before being ignited and causing a momentary brightness of the star. This process is similar to the Type Ia supernovae, but in the case of a nova the star is not destroyed. Another type of eruptive variable is based on the star R Coronae Borealis, which fades by a few magnitudes at fairly irregular intervals. The process behind the brightness drop is the expulsion of thick, almost soot-like, clouds of carbon in the atmosphere of the star and, over time, it gradually returns to normal brightness as the pressure from the energy emitted causes the clouds to disperse.

Whatever the cause for the change in brightness of the variable stars, the principle

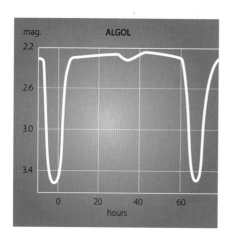

◀ *Measuring the brightness of variable stars like Algol in Perseus allows their light curve to be plotted.*

► *Variable-star comparison charts help the observer to estimate their brightness.*

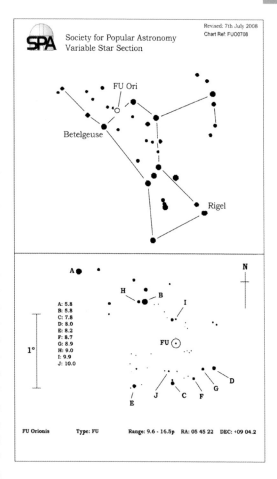

of observing them remains the same and it is a skill that will improve over time. Observations can either be made of the few naked-eye variable stars if you do not have any equipment or of the many hundreds and thousands of binocular or telescopic ones. Whichever ones you choose to observe, the first step is to get hold of comparison charts for the area.

These are charts that are centred on the variable star and are annotated with the brightnesses of non-variable stars surrounding it, and from them you can estimate the brightness of the variable star. The first step is to find two stars which lie in the same field of view, one a little brighter than the variable star you are observing and one which is a little fainter. By looking at the two comparison stars, decide whether your target star is exactly halfway in brightness between the other two stars. If it is, then it is easy to estimate its magnitude based on the magnitude of the other two; for example, if the two stars are magnitude 3 and magnitude 4, and the target is about halfway between them, then you can estimate its brightness at 3.5. However, it will not always be quite so obvious and it may be a little nearer the brightness of one compared to the other, so you will need to adjust your estimate accordingly. You can look for other companion stars which are of similar brightness to your estimated variable-star brightness, and from this you can tweak the brightness estimate you have come up with. With practice you can get surprisingly accurate results. In this way, you can build up a chart showing how the star brightness has varied over time or you can submit your brightness estimate to one of the many organizations like the American Association of Variable Star Observers (AAVSO) to combine your results with those of other observers around the world.

As with the other projects already covered, it is possible to use CCD cameras and software to measure precisely the brightness of the star, but this is a little more time-consuming and the equipment can be costly. Visual observations are easy and, providing time is spent being certain you are looking in the right portion of the sky, you are sure to get results and improve accuracy with practice.

Monitoring active galactic nuclei

Another project which is very similar in practice to observing variable stars is the study of active galactic nuclei (AGN). As the name suggests, an active galactic nucleus is the region at the centre of a galaxy that has a higher-than-usual energy profile, kicking out far more energy than their non-active counterparts. Before the identification of their true nature, these star-like objects were simply thought to be faint stars rather than superluminous objects at the far reaches of the Universe. We now think that supermassive black holes are the driving force behind the active cores, where material is being sucked into the black hole, but before finally passing the event horizon where it will disappear from view, the material forms a rotating accretion disk of material which travels faster nearer the centre. As material spins around towards its ultimate demise, frictional forces cause the material to heat to temperatures high enough to cause them to emit radiation at nearly all wavelengths of the electromagnetic spectrum. It is this radiation which can be detected by Earth-based telescopes, even those owned by amateur astronomers.

There are two types of active galaxies: those which are considered to be radio quiet and those which are radio loud, relating to the emission chiefly in the radio wavelengths from jets that seem to spring from the rotational axis of the black hole. Among the class of radio-quiet galaxies are the well-known Seyfert galaxies and quasars, with blazars being the most well known of the radio-loud category. There are other types of active galaxy among these two distinct groups but it is now thought that they actually represent the same object, just viewed from a different angle. When viewed face-on they can appear

▲ *An artist's impression of a black hole with material spiralling in around an accretion disk.*

▲ *Simulation of the jet emitted from an active galaxy. It is their orientation, or more accurately of their jets, which determines how we see them.*

most luminous; however, when viewed edge-on the obscuring dust of the galaxy and accretion disk can decrease the amount of radiation we can detect.

Due to the vast distances involved, the intense radiation from the AGNs actually appears quite faint in the sky so it is a project best left to those that own an astronomical telescope of at least 20 cm aperture. The purpose of studying AGNs is to help understand their nature, as they still hold some mysteries. The observations centre around three objectives: to monitor the apparent change in brightness, to build up an accurate light curve in visible light, and to act as an alerting mechanism to larger professional observatories in order to study strange behaviour as soon as possible at close quarters.

Observations of AGNs use the same set of skills as observing variable stars, as the key information required is an estimate of the brightness. Most AGNs are almost stellar in appearance so comparisons are drawn between the brightness of the AGN and of nearby comparison stars, but special charts are needed because their brightness is usually below the brightness covered by most star charts. The charts can be acquired from organizations such as *The Astronomer*, and from these it is possible to estimate the brightness of the AGN. Observations are then submitted to professional organizations and combined with those from other amateur astronomers around the world to build a light curve.

Recording astronomical objects

For many people, looking at astronomical objects is not enough and attention soon turns to trying to record what can be seen. Some people try drawing, which is a great way of learning to see more. This may sound strange, but an experienced observer will see more through a telescope than a newcomer who has never looked through a telescope before. Drawing what you can see through a telescope will make you look in a much more focused way and it requires nothing more than a set of pencils, an eraser, some paper and a red torch. Make sure you get a range of pencils of varying 'hardness', with the harder pencils ideal for stars and detail, and the softer pencils great for subtle wispy detail like clouds and nebulosity.

Prepare for your first drawing by taking a plain sheet of white paper and draw a circle in the centre about 5 cm in diameter. You do not need to be too specific about the size – it is easier just to find a glass or a cup which is about the right size and draw round that. To start your first drawing, centre the object in the field of view of the eyepiece and spend a few minutes just looking at it – do not try and draw it yet. Then, when you have studied its size, shape and appearance, take your paper (which should ideally be on a clipboard that has a red light attached to it) and draw in the brightest stars. Make the dots for these stars a little larger than the dots for the fainter stars. Once you have marked the positions of the stars, you can then start to sketch the outline of the object you are looking at, slowly working from the bigger obvious features to the smaller less obvious ones. Correct any mistakes or add highlights with the eraser and you can use your finger to smudge to give a little more subtlety to nebulosity. Keep checking back at the eyepiece as you draw and compare your final result with the view. Similar principles apply to drawing planets except that the circle becomes the disk of the planet and you simply draw the features that you can see, starting with the largest and working down to the smallest.

▲ *Drawing astronomical objects is not only good fun but it really helps to hone your observing skills.*

▲ *Star trails are a great first project for the budding astronomical photographer and only require a DSLR, tripod and remote control.*

Another option is to use digital cameras to capture what you can see. Some truly beautiful shots can be achieved by using a standard DSLR, fitting it to a tripod, pointing it at the sky and opening the shutter for an hour or so. The trick here is to close the aperture of the lens down one stop from fully open to help get nice sharp star images, and set the film speed to about 200 ISO and the exposure to 'B'. You will need a way of remotely operating the shutter so you do not make the camera shake when taking the picture, or you can place a piece of card over the lens while you push the button, wait for the shake to die down, then remove the card and reverse this procedure at the end of the exposure. With this technique you will get stunning star trails as the Earth spins, causing the light from the stars to produce curved streaks of light in the picture (see page 142 for more tips).

If you shorten the exposure to just 30 seconds or so, depending on the focal length of the camera lens (longer-focal-length lenses require shorter exposures) and the area of sky being photographed (shorter exposures nearer the celestial equator), then you can capture the stars as pinpricks rather than streaks and record them as constellations. You might also pick up the beauty of the Milky Way so it is worth experimenting with exposures and lenses to see what you can get.

For close-up shots, though, you need to use a telescope, which makes the job a whole lot more fiddly because the telescope acts like a really long focal-length lens. So that you do not capture the rotation of the Earth and subsequent blurring of the picture, exposure times of less than a second are needed. Unless you are trying to capture the Moon, exposures of that length will not be long enough. The solution is to use a telescope with a drive system, such as the equatorially driven telescopes we looked at in Chapter 3. DSLR cameras are increasingly popular but great planetary images can be gained by using webcams. By simply removing the lens of

◀ *Using tracking camera platforms helps to freeze the rotation of Earth, allowing you to get sharp constellation pictures like this shot of Orion.*

▶ *The Plough in Ursa Major is a great pointer to Polaris for polar alignment.*

▼ *Cassiopeia is brought to life with the stars of the Milky Way in the background.*

a webcam, it is possible to fit an adaptor to it that will allow it to slot into the eyepiece holder of a telescope. The webcam then records a video of the planet which is made up of hundreds of individual pictures. These can then all be added together or stacked

◄ *Webcams allow you to remove the distorting effects of the atmosphere on planetary pictures.*

▼ *DSLR or CCD cameras can reveal deep-sky objects in glorious colour, such as the Trapezium Cluster in the Orion Nebula.*

by free software available off the internet to produce planetary images of high quality. Using this technique enables the random movement of the atmosphere to be eradicated, leaving you with a beautiful sharp picture.

To try and record deep-space objects through a telescope requires more effort, and although DSLR cameras can give some great results, the more specialist astronomy cameras known as CCDs will give much better results. You must be careful to choose a camera that fits with the optical specifications of your telescope to get the best results. There is an in-depth section about this in *Philip's Astrophotography with Mark Thompson*. You can also choose between one-shot colour cameras which, as their name suggests, give you a colour picture from one exposure, or you can get a black-and-white camera and use a filter wheel system through which you take red, green and blue images and then combine them to make a colour picture.

Getting the digital picture, be it through a camera on a tripod or a webcam or a CCD through a telescope, is just the beginning as you will now need to process the image to get the best out of it. More work is required for images with exposures longer than a few seconds as they can suffer with electrical noise, which manifests itself as tiny dots over your picture. To get rid of this noise it is necessary to take an additional picture known as a 'dark frame', where you take an exposure of the same length of time but with the end of the telescope covered over. This effectively allows you to capture the noise in a picture which you can then subtract away from the image of the object you wish to photograph. All this effort is worthwhile though, and you will be treated with some beautiful records of the objects you have observed.

Useful organizations

There are many organizations out there that can help you get started with some of these projects and a few are listed here:

- The Society for Popular Astronomy is great for newcomers, with active observing groups – www.popastro.co.uk
- The British Astronomical Association has a very active set of observing groups – www.britastro.org
- The American Association of Variable Star Observers is the organization that compiles observations from groups around the world – www.aavso.org
- The Central Bureau for Astronomical Telegrams is associated with the International Astronomical Union and is the organization to which discoveries should be reported – www.cbat.eps.harvard.edu/index.html
- *The Astronomer* publishes information about astronomical discoveries and provides lots of useful information for those wishing to take part in observational projects – www.theastronomer.org

HOW TO TAKE STUNNING STAR TRAIL IMAGES

The previous few pages explained a technique for capturing star trails that involves using a single long exposure. One of the difficulties with this method is that a long exposure not only captures extra stars and the rotation of the Earth but it also enhances the brightness of the sky. If the exposure is too long and there is a good amount of light in the sky, then you may find that your lovely night-time shot resembles broad daylight and the stars are no longer visible. Fortunately, there is an alternative way of capturing star trails that takes a little more work but the rewards are worth it.

More cameras are suited to this alternative technique as exposures are limited to about 30 seconds instead of many minutes or even hours. A wide-angle lens is ideal for capturing large areas of the sky but the camera still needs to be securely mounted to a tripod or other fixed rigid support and focused on the stars. With a DSLR camera, this in itself can be challenging as it will be very unlikely that you can see anything through the viewfinder. Set the focus of the camera to 'infinity' and then point it at the sky in the direction of Polaris. In the northern hemisphere, this region of the sky moves the least so it is a great place to take test exposures for focus. Set the aperture to one stop less than fully open – the f/number will vary depending on the lens you have but with a wide-angle lens this will usually be around f/5.6 or thereabouts. Now set the ISO to around 6400 and the exposure to about 10 seconds. Finally, with a remote control, take one shot and look at the resultant picture. If no stars are visible, try improving the sensitivity by increasing the ISO setting or slightly extending the exposure time. Once you can see stars, use the camera controls to zoom in on them to check

they are nice and sharp. All of this effort is time well spent as I have found that some lenses are not focused at infinity even when they say they are! It is best to check, so tweak the focus if necessary to get a nice sharp star.

Now that your camera is focused, leave everything set as is but change the exposure time to about 30 seconds. The next thing to consider is the framing of the shot. Star trails can look beautifully enhanced if you can get a nice bit of foreground in the shot, so consider trying to get a tree or a building in the frame. For this to be visible you will either need to take one exposure with the flash to illuminate it or you could try waving a torch over it during one of the exposures. Then, with the scene shot all lined up, we get to the clever bit!

Some cameras have the ability to take multiple exposures, as do many of the remote controls available. You will need to check how to configure your camera or remote control to take multiple exposures and set it to take as many shots as you like of 30 seconds' duration. The more individual

shots you take, the longer the star trails will be. Start off with 60 shots of 30 seconds to see what the result is. If your system allows you to put a delay between images, then set that to zero otherwise your star trails will end up looking like dashed lines. Now it is time to start the exposures, sit back and wait. If you are taking 60 images of 30 seconds each, then this will take half an hour to run through.

When the camera has finished taking all the shots, you now need to connect the camera to your computer and add all of the individual pictures together. You will need to download software to do this and there are loads of different pieces of free software available. Search for 'star trail stacking software' and choose one for your operating system. Load up the software and your individual images. There may be a few configuration issues for this, but star trail tracking software is pretty simple and straightforward to use. With your images loaded, click on the button for stacking them all together and watch the magic as your individual star pictures turn into one beautiful star trail image.

Don't be frightened to experiment with this technique. Try higher ISO sensitivity to capture more stars or slightly longer exposures. If you can plug your camera into a power source then try taking hundreds of images to get longer trails. You can also try pointing at different regions of the sky to see how that affects the trails. If you want to learn other techniques for imaging the sky then check out *Philip's Astrophotography with Mark Thompson*.

chapter 7

INTRODUCING THE UNIVERSE

WHEN I STARTED astronomy as a young lad of ten I enjoyed discovering new worlds and distant star systems that I had never seen before. As the years passed I wanted to learn more about the objects I was looking at, until I find myself in a place now where I get a real sense of fascination by knowing the science behind the objects I'm studying. It is very easy to get lost in the equipment and gadgets or observing techniques, but in reality astronomy, for me at least, is about the objects. This chapter is all about them, the objects that make up our night sky, and I hope that, by including them, they help to bring more to your enjoyment of the Universe.

We start by looking at the closest of our astronomical neighbours, the **Moon**. Most people recognize it and are familiar with its phases and craters, but not so many understand the true nature of them nor indeed the nature of the Moon itself. We now think that the Moon formed when the Earth was still young, probably just under 5 billion years ago, and

the most popular theory suggests that a huge object crashed into fledgling Earth, sending debris high into orbit. Over millions of years, the heavier elements settled back down on to Earth, while the lighter elements stayed in orbit and slowly, under the force of gravity, were pulled together to form the Moon we see today.

Like all objects in the young, turbulent Solar System, the Moon became subject to bombardment from debris left over from the formation of the Solar System. The lack of an atmosphere meant that even the smallest fragments got through, crashing into the surface and leaving behind craters as evidence of the impacts. It is a different story here on Earth because the atmosphere protects us from impacts of the smaller pieces of rock. Instead of striking the surface, they burn up high in the

◀ *Lunar surface detail is really obvious along the terminator – look at the detail in this image of the five-day-old Moon.*

▶ *Copernicus is a beautiful example of a lunar crater, measuring 93 kilometres in diameter.*

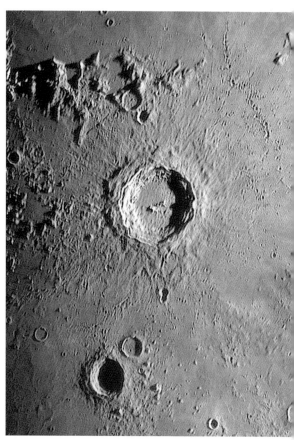

atmosphere (shooting stars), but the larger chunks can survive the fiery plunge and fall to Earth. It is an impact like this that is thought to have been the cause of the dinosaurs' demise millions of years ago.

Taking a close look at the craters on the Moon is a rewarding activity and a great range of features can be seen around them. Most of them are circular in shape due to the impact throwing material or ejecta out in all directions (although it is not the shape of the impactor which causes the common circular crater shape). There are a few craters, however, that have a slightly elongated appearance, which may be the result of a glancing blow from an incoming chunk of rock, but perhaps more curious are the crater chains such as the Davey Crater chain. This feature is best seen at high magnifications when the Moon is about eight days old and is thought to have been caused by ejecta having been thrown out from a meteorite impact, which then caused secondary impacts. We can see evidence for this in the shape of the secondary craters and disturbances around their rims, suggesting a very low impact angle. Another possible explanation for those with a slightly different appearance is the result of a cometary impact, and we saw evidence of this in July 1994 when Comet Shoemaker–Levy 9 was broken apart by tidal forces before colliding with Jupiter. It is now thought that similarly fragmented comets impacting the lunar surface could be the cause of other crater chains.

Another nice feature of many craters that you can look out for are the central peaks, which are the result of the high energy released during an impact event. The high energy temporarily melts the surface material and the force of the impact causes it to spread out towards the edge of the crater. The 'sloshy' material will only go so far before rebounding and heading back towards the middle of the crater, where it produces a peak in the centre before slowly solidifying. Take a look at the craters down the line between day and night on the Moon, known as the terminator, to try and spot one of these lunar peaks.

On Earth, we have an atmosphere which erodes away evidence of all but the largest impact craters, but it is a different story on the Moon. We can clearly see the result of this cratering all over the lunar surface, and by studying the distribution, sizes and overlapping

Mark's lunar observing tip

The best place to look to see detail on the Moon is down the line between the dark and light sections. It is called the *terminator* and is the point where shadows on the Moon are longest and surface features are more enhanced. The full Moon is the worst time to try and observe its features as there is no terminator visible and shadows are minimal.

of them it is possible to determine the age of the surface and hence the age of the Moon. Looking at the Moon, even with the naked eye, reveals that there are other strange features visible that look like vast plains. Ancient astronomers thought they looked like seas, hence they got the name 'Maria' from the Latin word for 'sea'. But even telescopic observation through modest instruments reveals that these plains are just that, and studying their shape and boundaries shows that they too were once craters. Millions of years ago there were many more larger pieces of rock rattling around the Solar System, and when they crashed into the lunar surface the resultant impacts cracked and penetrated the crust. This allowed molten lava to seep up from below, filling the newly formed giant craters, and over time this lava solidified, giving the Moon the appearance we see today.

A less well understood feature is the transient lunar phenomenon, which has been recorded on many occasions over the last thousand years by professional and amateur astronomers alike. As the name suggests, these events are short-lived, almost fleeting, and appear as brief flashes of light or glows against the lunar landscape. I have observed the night sky for nearly 30 years and the Moon has been a big part of that, but I have never seen any of them. That is not to say they do not exist though, as some events have been seen by more than one observer. Their origins are still unknown, although among the common theories they are thought to be simply flashes due to meteorite impact or outgassing of trapped gases from beneath the lunar surface.

One of the more recognizable and very well understood lunar phenomena is its

constantly changing appearance, which we call the phases. We only see the Moon because it reflects sunlight – turn the Sun off, and the Moon would seem to vanish. The phases of the Moon change because the relative position of the Sun and Moon change with respect to the Earth. When the Moon lies opposite the Sun in the sky, we see the fully illuminated portion and experience a full Moon, and when it lies between the Sun and the Earth, we see the

◄ *Clavius is one of the largest craters on the Moon, measuring 255 kilometres from one edge to the other.*

▶ *We see the Moon because it reflects sunlight. The changing relative positions of the Earth, Moon and Sun give rise to the changing phases of the Moon as seen from Earth. When the Moon lies between the Earth and Sun (new Moon) we see the non-illuminated hemisphere, but when the Earth is between the Moon and Sun (full Moon) we see the fully illuminated hemisphere. Between new Moon and full Moon are varying degrees of illumination.*

non-illuminated portion which we call a new Moon. At varying points between these we see the illuminated portion of the Moon get slowly bigger and then slowly smaller. One full lunar cycle of phases takes about a month, hence the origins of the word 'month', from the word 'Moon'.

It would be reasonable to think that when we have a new Moon and it sits between us and the Sun, that it would block the Sun from our view. Using the same logic, you would think at full Moon that the Earth would block sunlight from reaching the Moon, so it would go dark. It turns out that the shape and orientation of the orbit of the Moon means it sometimes sits just above and sometimes just below the line between the Sun and Earth. As we saw in Chapter 2, there are occasions when the three align perfectly and it is at these times that we see eclipses. Lunar eclipses occur when the Moon passes into the shadow cast by the Earth and solar eclipses occur when the Moon blocks sunlight from reaching a tiny portion of the Earth. When lunar eclipses occur you can see them from anywhere on the Earth that you can see the Moon, but to see a solar eclipse you need to be in the path of the eclipse, which is a tiny portion of the Earth, so in reality the solar eclipses are much rarer.

As the month progresses and the phases continue along their cycle, you may have noticed that we always seem to see the same hemisphere of the Moon. This is a phenomenon called 'tidal locking' and it is caused by the force of gravity from the Earth and Moon pulling on one another. The pull causes a bulge to appear on each body, which acts as a braking motion on the Moon's rotation to such an extent that it takes the Moon the same length of time to rotate once on its axis as it takes to orbit once around the Earth. We now see the same hemisphere of the Moon facing the Earth at all times, so there is about half of the Moon that we can never see from Earth. It is actually just less than half – around 41% of the lunar surface cannot be seen due to the shape of the Moon's orbit. You may have heard mention of 'the dark side of the Moon', but there is no dark side, only a far side – all portions of the Moon receive light and dark at some point.

Moving on from the Moon, we head to the inner reaches of our Solar System and to the star that gives us the heat and light we need to survive, the **Sun**. Many people take it for granted – it rises in the east and sets in the west – but without it we would not even be here, for its energy was instrumental, if not crucial, to the evolution of life on Earth.

All stars, the Sun included, live and die, and it is estimated that the Sun formed around 5 billion years ago out of a vast cloud of hydrogen gas and dust called a nebula. As the cloud collapsed under the force of gravity, the pressures became so intense that hydrogen atoms started crashing together in a process known as *fusion*. The solar fusion of hydrogen atoms produced helium atoms and the heat and light we experience from the Sun today. The nuclear reactions have been going on deep in its core ever since and, fortunately, there is enough material in the Sun for it to remain relatively stable for the next 5 billion years. It takes about a million years for the heat and light to escape from inside the dense Sun, before taking just over 8 minutes to reach us here on Earth, around 150 million km away. As the Sun evolves, the core will turn into a growing sphere of helium, but the temperatures will not be high enough for helium fusion to take place so the Sun will

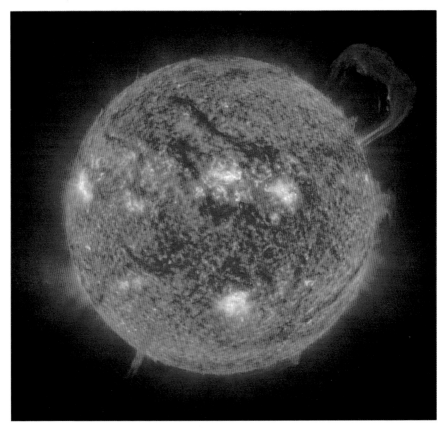

▲ *Solar prominences can be seen when the Sun is studied in different wavelengths, like this image taken by the SOHO spacecraft in September 1999.*

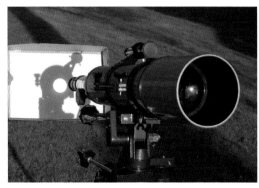

▶ *Solar projection allows you to look safely at the Sun, but do remember to keep the lens caps on the finder telescope.*

not be generating energy. The lack of energy production in the core means no outwards pressure to balance gravity, so it will start to contract. The contraction will cause the core to heat up, which will initiate the burning of a shell of hydrogen surrounding it. The new phase of hydrogen burning will cause it to swell, but as it swells the outer layers will start to cool again, turning it into a red-giant star. The helium core will continue to collapse until the temperatures are high enough to initiate helium fusion into carbon and oxygen. The temperatures in the core of the Sun will never get high enough to initiate carbon fusion so this will mark the beginning of the end of the Sun's life, which will eventually lose its outer layers into space as a planetary nebula.

When studied with specialist equipment, the Sun is revealed in its true nature as a vast seething ball of gas with eruptions blasting out of the visible surface. Studying it in normal 'white' light reveals strange spots on the surface called *sunspots*, which are magnetic disturbances in the gas. They can be studied over months and years and patterns can be seen emerging, such as the well-understood 11-yearly sunspot cycle. Sunspots can easily be seen by projecting an image of the Sun as detailed in my 'solar observing tip' below, or through the use of full-aperture solar filters as discussed in Chapter 5 (see page 115). If you do invest in the more expensive H-alpha filter systems or dedicated solar telescopes, you will be amazed at the detail you can see, with solar flares and prominences among the stunning objects on show. If you watch them over a period of time, you will see how their appearance slowly changes.

Mark's solar observing tip

The easiest and safest way to observe the Sun is to project an image of it through binoculars or a telescope. Point at the Sun **WITHOUT** looking through (you can get lined up by looking at the shadow on the ground – when it's at its smallest it is pointing at the Sun), then place a piece of white card about a foot away from the eyepiece and you will see a projected image of the Sun on the card. Don't place the card too close as there is still enough heat to burn the card. **DO NOT** leave the telescope or binoculars pointing at the Sun for more than a few minutes as the intense heat can cause the glue and plastic parts inside to melt. If you have a telescope larger than 4 inches then you should make a cardboard mask with a hole cut into it about 3 or 4 inches in diameter and place it over the front end of the telescope to cut down the amount of light that enters. **Never, ever look directly at the Sun!**

The visible surface of the Sun upon which sunspots can be seen is called the *photosphere*, and it is surrounded by the *chromosphere*, where all the eruptions called prominences and flares occur. This is in turn surrounded by the rather more difficult to study *corona*, which is only visible with professional equipment or during solar eclipses.

One very key and important point to remember with the Sun is **NEVER** to observe it directly either with or without optical aid. It can and will cause blindness. You can find details of how to observe the Sun safely in my tip on the previous page.

It is really hard to appreciate the full enormity of the Sun as it lies so far from us. However, it is so large that you could fit just over 1 million planet Earths inside it! With all the activity on the Sun, it is no surprise that this giant object sometimes has a big impact on us here on Earth. The prominences and flares are examples of the way the Sun throws off material out into the Solar System. On occasions the material is thrown towards the Earth, and when it arrives it can knock out communications satellites and other technology, causing wide-scale disruption. Amongst the chaos it can cause, it can also give rise to the most amazing and beautiful auroral displays, which can be seen around the polar regions on most nights and on few occasions nearer to the Equator (see page 72).

Moving outwards from the Sun brings us to the **inner planets**, Mercury and Venus, and because they are closer to the Sun than us they are never far from it in the sky. Mercury is the nearest to the Sun, at an average distance of 58 million km. It has a very slow rotation, which results in the daytime side roasting in temperatures of around 465°C, but due to its very thin atmosphere the night-time side plummets to −184°C. The lack of atmosphere means that the surface of Mercury has not been protected from the constant pounding from meteoroids so its surface resembles that of the Moon, peppered by craters. It orbits the Sun taking 88 Earth days to complete one orbit, and for every two full orbits it will have completed three revolutions on its axis. This means that from

◄ *Mariner 10 took this image of Mercury just after its closest approach. It is a mosaic of 18 images which show the planet's surface in incredible detail.*

▶ *The Pioneer spacecraft revealed amazing detail in the clouds of Venus. The clouds are highly reflective, making Venus one of the brightest objects in our sky.*

the surface of Mercury an observer would see the Sun rise and set once in a two-year period (that is, based on a year defined by Mercury's orbit, not an Earth year).

In contrast to Mercury, Venus has a very dense carbon dioxide atmosphere which has protected it from all but the largest meteoric impacts. The dense atmosphere has another effect too – it serves as an insulation blanket! The heat and energy from the Sun passes through the thick Venusian atmosphere, heats up the surface and then gets reradiated at a slightly different wavelength. This reradiated energy is unable to escape through the thick atmosphere so the planet gets warmer and warmer. The average temperature on Venus is a staggering 449°C and the presence of the atmosphere means the night-time side is not much cooler than the daytime.

Spacecraft that have visited both of these two planets have recorded pretty hostile conditions. The Venera landers which visited Venus recorded the high surface temperatures, but also detected sulphuric acid rain and an atmospheric pressure around 90 times the atmospheric pressure we experience on Earth. As a result of the different geology and atmospheric conditions, the surface topography is very different between the two: Mercury is covered with craters, but the surface of Venus is scarred by evidence of a very geologically active past, with volcanoes, vast canyons and solidified lava flows.

Trying to look at these two objects through telescopes is challenging, and in fact the only useful thing that can be picked out from telescopic ground-based observation is the phase. In the case of Venus, it is occasionally possible to pick out atmospheric detail but very good sky conditions must exist, plus excellent optics and an experienced eye will be needed. The highly reflective atmosphere of Venus is one of the reasons it appears so bright in the sky.

We have already looked at solar eclipses where the Moon passes directly between the Earth and the Sun, blocking it from our view, but there are occasions when either of the two inner planets can also pass directly in front of the Sun, though due to the orientation of the orbits these events are rare. They are known as *transits* – the last transit of Mercury was in 2006, with the next occurring on 9 May 2016, but much less frequent are the transits of Venus, of which we only have about 15 per century. The last transit of Venus was seen in

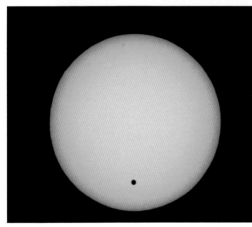

▲ *Not only does Venus display an almost full set of phases but it also changes in size quite significantly as its distance to our own planet varies.*

◀ *The transit of Venus on 8 June 2004, when Venus passed directly in between the Earth and Sun, gave amateur astronomers a chance to witness the rare event. The next transit visible from Europe is in December 2125!*

June 2012 and it is a long wait to the next one in December 2117, which will be visible only around the Pacific. European observers must wait until 8 December 2125! Although it is a bit of a wait, the safest way to observe transits like these is with solar-projection techniques or full-aperture solar filters.

Transits occur when the inner planets are at a position known as *inferior conjunction*, which means they lie between the Earth and the Sun. When they lie on the far side of the Sun they are said to be at *superior conjunction* – planets at this position are impossible to see.

Mark's inner planet observing tip

The best time to observe the two innermost planets is when they appear to be at the most extreme points in their orbit as viewed from Earth. These points are known as greatest eastern or western elongation depending on which side of the Sun they are. When they are at this point, they will appear to be at the greatest distance from the Sun in the sky and so easier than usual to spot. Mercury is the most elusive of the two, but both planets will only ever be visible in the evening or morning skies, never in the depths of the night.

Any planet which orbits the Sun beyond the orbit of Earth is considered to be an **outer planet**. The major planets now only include Mars, Jupiter, Saturn, Uranus and Neptune. Pluto was dethroned as a planet back in 2006 by the International Astronomical Union (IAU) and now comes under the category of a minor planet, along with a whole host of other small rocky bodies.

Mars is probably the closest planet we have that resembles Earth. Over the decades that astronomers have been observing the 'Red Planet' there have often been rumours that life exists there, but this has its roots in mankind's overactive imagination. To date, we know of no firm evidence of life on Mars – however, NASA's Curiosity Mars rover identified that the Martian atmosphere was once capable of supporting life, though whether it ever did is another matter.

As a planet, Mars is the second smallest and is about half the size of Earth, with a diameter of about 6,500 km. It orbits the Sun once every 686 Earth days, which means it is only very well placed for observation once every two years. Between those times, it is often visible but very small in the sky so little detail can be seen. We have learned lots about the Red Planet from visiting spacecraft ever since the 1970s, when the Viking landers became

▲ *Mars as seen through the Hubble Space Telescope reveals amazing surface and atmospheric detail.*

the first man-made visitors. However, it is not just visiting spacecraft that have made discoveries – back in August 1877 Asaph Hall discovered two moons in orbit around Mars, known as Phobos and Deimos. Both are pretty faint, though, and require telescopes of at least 15 cm aperture to detect.

When you look at Mars telescopically, its red colour becomes more apparent although it actually looks a little more pink than red. The colour is caused by the presence of iron oxide, a fine dusty material that covers the Martian surface. Closer study will reveal polar ice caps that are made of carbon dioxide ice, a colossal volcano called Olympus Mons that dwarfs any volcano here on Earth, and a valley system called Valles Marineris that makes the Grand Canyon on Earth look like a tiny crack!

Beyond Mars is a belt of asteroids that separates the small rocky planets from the large gaseous ones. The belt contains hundreds of thousands of asteroids, although, surprisingly, nearly half of its mass is found within its four largest ones: Ceres, Pallas, Vesta and Hygiea. The impression given of the asteroid belt by science-fiction movies is that flying through it is a dangerous occupation, but due to the vastness of space the component asteroids are separated by considerable distance and you would probably not even see one if you decided to fly through it. A number of asteroids are visible to the amateur astronomer and I recall one such asteroid, although not from the asteroid belt, I hasten to add, which passed between the Earth and the Moon. It was incredible to see it slowly drifting through space.

Beyond the asteroid belt and heading on our journey out of the Solar System we come to the largest of all the planets, Jupiter, at an average distance of 700 million km from the Sun. Like the rest of the giant planets, Jupiter is a big ball of gas and all we can see from Earth is the top of its atmosphere. It may have a liquid metal core but there is no solid surface like the small rocky planets of the inner Solar System. Jupiter has a pretty striking appearance, covered in a complex system of belts and bands, all of which are the

▲ *The Cassini spacecraft visited Jupiter on its way to Saturn in December 2000 and took this stunning image.*

▲ *This image of Jupiter and three of the Galilean satellites (from left to right, Ganymede, Europa and Io) was taken through an amateur telescope.*

▲ *Io is the innermost of the Galilean satellites.*

▲ *Ganymede is the largest moon in the Solar System.*

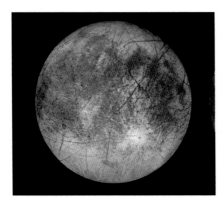

▲ *Europa is a frozen world believed to have a subsurface ocean.*

▲ *Callisto is the second largest moon in the Jovian system.*

result of different gases in the atmosphere. The most prominent features are the north and south equatorial belts, which run either side of its equator, but look closely in the southern one and you will see the Great Red Spot which is a hurricane system that has been raging for hundreds of years. This can easily be seen in amateur telescopes due to its colossal size – almost three Earths would fit inside it! It is also possible to see belts in the upper layers which are the result of different gases and the wind systems found in the upper atmosphere.

Telescopic observations of Jupiter will also show up some of its moons, four of which were discovered by Galileo when he first turned a telescope to the sky over 400 years ago – Io, Europa, Ganymede and Callisto. It was the observation of the moons of Jupiter that led to the first estimates of the speed of light, but it began with attempts to determine longitude at sea. Galileo suggested that the movement of the moons of Jupiter could be used as a celestial clock, and that by observing them at sea, longitude could be determined. This turned out to be impractical due to the difficulties in making telescopic observations on the moving deck of a ship. However, working with Italian astronomer Giovanni Cassini and Frenchman Jean Picard to fine-tune the determination of longitude from observations of Jupiter's moons was a Danish astronomer called Ole Rømer. Rømer noticed that there seemed to be differences between the predicted times of various eclipses of the moons and the actual observed times. He deduced that these differences were the direct result of

▼ *Individual images are often combined in a mosaic like this picture of Saturn from Cassini. It was made of 126 individual images taken over two hours on 6 October 2004. Saturn was at a distance of 6.3 million km away.*

Mark's outer planet observing tip
The best time to observe the outer planets is when they are at opposition. That means they are opposite the Sun in the sky and so are at their closest to us and at their biggest. Features should be easiest to pick out when they are at this point in their orbit.

the extra time it was taking light to traverse the distance across the orbit of the Earth. In fact, it seemed to be taking 22 minutes to cross the orbit of the Earth, which led to the determination of the speed of light as 220,000 km/sec. This figure was announced back in 1676, which is impressively close to the modern-day value for the speed of light of 300,000 km/sec.

Saturn is the next planet from the Sun and is famous for its incredible ring system. Like Jupiter it is a large gas planet, measuring 116,000 km in diameter, but although it is about nine times the size of the Earth it is still dwarfed by Jupiter at nearly 143,000 km. Jupiter does have a set of rings but they are by no means as impressive as Saturn's which, while they look solid from Earth, are actually made up of billions of pieces of ice and rock all orbiting around the planet in the same way that our Moon orbits around Earth. Even through modest amateur telescopes, gaps can be seen in amongst the rings, like the famous Cassini Division that separates the A ring and B ring. The gaps are formed by a number of gravitational effects but the most common are the shepherd moons, larger chunks of rock which exert a gravitational pull on the ring particles, ensuring that they do not wander into the gaps. Saturn has larger moons which orbit outside the ring system, some of which can be seen with amateur telescopes and which, along with the shepherd moons, total more than 60!

Uranus and Neptune are the final two outer planets in our Solar System and can just be seen through binoculars and small telescopes. Both are known as ice giants due to the presence of ices, which do not exist in a solid state as you would expect. Unlike Jupiter and Saturn, which appear more creamy-brown in colour, Uranus and Neptune appear blue due to the presence of methane high in their atmospheres. The methane absorbs red light from the Sun but reflects the blue light, giving them their distinctive colour. Of the two planets, Neptune seems to display a few more features in its atmosphere, such as high-level cirrus clouds of methane crystals and giant dark hurricanes, like the Great Red Spot on Jupiter. Uranus is unique in the way it orbits the Sun. All of the planets orbit the

▶ *This image of Uranus was captured by Voyager 2 in January 1986 at a distance of 9.1 million km and shows the planet in true colour.*

▲ *Earth-like cirrus clouds of methane and the Great Dark Spot can be seen in the atmosphere of Neptune in this beautiful shot by Voyager 2 at a distance of 16 million km.*

Sun along a plane that we call the ecliptic. With respect to this ecliptic, all of the planets except Uranus spin on an axis that is near enough upright (although even Earth is tilted a little, by about 23°). Uranus, though, is tilted over on its axis by about 91°, so it is almost rolling around the Solar System. It is thought that this strange attitude is the result of an impact at some point in the young planet's life by a wayward asteroid or comet.

Beyond the orbit of the outer planets are a whole bunch of tiny objects that are often overlooked. Far beyond the orbit of Pluto, a group of minor Solar System bodies called the Oort Cloud play host to the **comets** that occasionally, and often unexpectedly, grace our skies.

It has to be said that comets are, at best, unpredictable. They orbit the Sun in the cold depths of the Solar System and have a composition much like that of a dirty snowball, with rock and ice as the main ingredients. Most cometary nuclei will lie dormant for millions of years, but occasional collisions within the orbiting clouds will send a comet towards the inner Solar System. They warm up as they fall closer to the Sun, and as their temperature rises, so the ice melts. Because of the conditions in space, the ice does not turn to liquid; instead, it turns straight to a gas in a process called *sublimation*. This then becomes a vast cloud called a *coma*, measuring millions of kilometres, surrounding the tiny solid nucleus.

▶ *Comet Hale–Bopp (C/1995 01) enthralled skywatchers across the globe in 1997. This image clearly reveals the blue ion tail and the white dust tail.*

A nearly constant stream of pressure from the Sun, called the *solar wind*, pushes against the coma, producing the trademark tail of the comet. It is interesting to note that the tail of the comet always points away from the Sun – it has nothing to do with the comet's direction of motion. With particularly bright and spectacular comets, it is possible to see not just one but two tails, one made of dust that has been dislodged from the nucleus and one made of gas from the sublimated ice. The tails tend to separate as the dust particles are affected more by the force of gravity and curve away, separating them where the atoms of gas remain pointing away from the Sun. Comet Hale–Bopp, which was seen in 1997, was a fine example of a comet with two tails, clearly visible to the naked eye from a dark site.

Very often new comets are seen just months or weeks before they become easily visible and many of them require telescopes to detect even at their brightest. There are a number of well-known comets that return regularly after a number of years and are called short-period comets, whilst occasionally big bright ones suddenly appear, taking us all by surprise before heading back to the depths of the Solar System for thousands of years. This latter type are known as long-period comets and tend to be the more spectacular ones. As comets orbit the Sun and they shed material, their orbits become littered with their debris. If the Earth moves through this path of debris, it will sweep up the particles of rock which then fall to Earth, usually burning up high in the atmosphere. We see this demise as a meteor or shooting star, but each year we are treated to about 20 meteor showers as the Earth ploughs through the orbits of comets on its annual journey around the Sun.

Mark's comet observing tip

Comets can become quite bright and may even be visible to the unaided eye. They tend to be at their brightest when they are close to the Sun, so it is often best to study them when they are low in the sky in the east before sunrise or in the west after sunset. The brighter ones are best observed with the naked eye or binoculars, as the larger field of view gives a much more pleasing result than the close-up view through a telescope.

◀ *This image shows M3, a large globular cluster in Canes Venatici that contains hundreds of thousands of stars. Red-giant stars can be seen scattered through the cluster, giving us a clue that this object is old, estimated at 11.3 billion years.*

At some as yet unidentified distance from the Sun, the realm of the Solar System ceases and interstellar space begins. From this point for thousands of light years there will be **stars**, stars and yet more stars. With a typical dark sky, it's possible to see just over 4,000 of them with the naked eye, and it is perhaps surprising to learn that about half of the stars you can see are members of double or multiple star systems. Far from being just a load of tiny lights in the sky, stars are a fascinating class of object in their own right, and of course our local star, the Sun, gives us a great opportunity to study one close up.

The first thing you might notice when you look at stars is that they vary in colour. This is not an illusion, as their colour is closely related to their temperature. Imagine a hot metal poker in a fire – as it warms up it will glow red, yellow, white then blue, depending on its temperature. We could tell how hot the poker is by observing its colour, and in the same way we can look at the colour of a star and tell how hot it really is. If we study the light from the star with an instrument called a spectroscope we can even see what it is made of. By studying the light of stars, we can not only learn what they are made of but we can also accurately deduce their temperature, size and even age. In deducing the sizes of the stars, some have been discovered which vary, shrinking and growing over a very regular period, and the variation in their brightness can be clearly measured – these are called *variable stars*.

There are other types of variable stars whose brightness variation is driven by other processes; for example, members of binary star systems can dip in brightness as one star passes in front of the other. These systems where more than one star makes up the tiny speck of light that we see are surprisingly common in the Universe. These stellar systems make up

▶ *Hidden in the light from stars are dark lines known as absorption lines. These lines are present where atoms have absorbed light and they help us to understand what objects are made of.*

▲ *The Dumbbell Nebula is a dying star and a glimpse into the future to the fate that awaits our Sun.*

an estimated 50% of all stars in the sky and by studying their motion around each other we can work out many other physical characteristics.

All stars, including our Sun, will eventually die. The Sun was formed about 5 billion years ago and for most of its life will fuse hydrogen into helium deep in its core. After fusing helium into other elements, it will eventually come to the end of its life. The ultimate demise of all stars is determined by their mass, and for stars like our Sun, they will die in a relatively quiet manner, swelling up to a red-giant star before losing all outer layers to space. The core will be left behind intact, incredibly dense and fading away as a white dwarf, while the outer layers escape off into space producing beautiful planetary nebulae, such as the Dumbbell Nebula in Vulpecula or the Ring Nebula in Lyra.

For stars that are more massive, they end their lives in a much more explosive manner, blowing themselves to pieces. The core of these stars collapse catastrophically, causing a sudden and explosive burst of energy, making the star explode. These supernova events mark one of the most violent explosions in the Universe, and one star going supernova will often outshine all the stars in a galaxy put together. Not much is left behind of the original star other than the supercompressed core which, depending on the star's mass, will either

Mark's observing tip for stars

It is quite easy to pick out the colours of the stars with the naked eye and variable-star brightness can be observed quite readily. If you are trying to look for binary or multiple stars, you will need a telescope to help separate the individual stars. Chapter 3 looked at resolution and how a bigger telescope allows you to see finer levels of detail. This means a bigger telescope will enable you to separate the individual stars in a binary star system. Find out the resolution of your telescope in arc minutes or arc seconds, check back to Chapter 2 and find some binary or multiple stars whose separation is greater than your telescope resolution, and you should be able to see all the stars in the system.

become a neutron star or maybe even a rather strange object called a *black hole*. To understand black holes we need to understand something called escape velocity. On Earth, if I were to throw a ball upwards as hard as I could, it would ultimately fall back to Earth. But if I could throw it faster, at over 7 km/sec, then it would be travelling fast enough to escape the gravitational pull of the Earth and disappear off into space. At the centre of a black hole is an object so dense that its pull of gravity is so immense that its escape velocity is faster than the speed of light, which means that even light, travelling at 300,000 km/sec, is not going fast enough to escape. The tiny singularity which is the remains of the super-compressed core of the star is surrounded by a region of space within which nothing, not even light, can escape.

The lives of stars are inextricably linked to the beautiful and ghostly **nebulae** that pervade interstellar space. Stars are created from them as they collapse under the force of gravity, and stars create them when they eventually die. Cast your gaze around the sky on any night and you might be able to spot the odd star that looks just a little bit fuzzy – do not worry, it is not your eyes. This is the light from those hazy gas clouds scattered throughout the Galaxy and their name originates from Latin, literally meaning 'cloud'. Unlike the clouds here on Earth, which are made up of water droplets, the nebulae are made up of gas and dust.

If you are lucky enough to own a telescope or binoculars, try pointing them at a nebula such as the Great Orion Nebula in Orion and you will reveal delicate filaments and wispy structure that give them the fuzzy appearance. The Orion Nebula is a fine example and has a distinctive red-and-blue look in colour images, which is pretty typical of this type of emission nebula where hot young stars are starting to shine. If a nebula lies close to stars like this, then the energy from them is enough to cause the gas atoms to energize and start to shine, giving off their own light, hence the name *emission nebula*. For those that are a little too far from a star to cause it to glow, then we see the starlight reflected off the dust particles as a *reflection nebula*, giving it a distinctive blue colour.

It takes millions of years for gravity slowly to collapse the nebulae that are creating stars, and as the temperatures and pressures increase, the crucial nuclear fusion processes start. Inside the Orion Nebula a number of stars have started to shine and you can see some of them through telescopes in the centre of the cloud. The cluster is known as the Trapezium and even small telescopes will reveal it. Over many millions of years, the remaining material in the nebula will slowly get blown away into the depths of space, eventually coming together again to form more new stars.

Not all nebulae on view are the result of stellar birth – some are the result of the death of stars such as the stunning *planetary nebulae*, which do look a little like planets through small telescopes. For much of a star's life, the force of gravity trying to collapse it is perfectly balanced by a force generated during the fusion process, known as the thermonuclear force, and it is at this stage that the star spends most of its life.

Those clouds that haven't yet collapsed enough to start the nuclear process of stellar birth, nor are related to the end of a star's life, may appear as dark clouds lurking in space. The only way to see them visually is if they are silhouetted against background stars or nebulae. You can see examples of these with the naked eye if you cast your eyes along the Milky Way from a dark site. There will be dark patches that are the result of these dark clouds, but perhaps the best known example of a dark nebula is found close to the Orion Nebula called the Horsehead Nebula. Large telescopes are needed to have any hope of seeing this

▲ *The stellar nurseries in Orion have examples of emission (red) and reflection (blue) nebulosity.*

▲ *The Horsehead Nebula is a difficult object to observe visually but an impressive object when caught on camera. The dusty nature of the cloud forming the horse's head is clear in this image.*

Mark's nebulae observing tip

Nebulae can be stunning through telescopes, but do not expect to see them as they appear in pictures. Cameras are much better than our eyes at detecting colour when light levels are low, so when you look at nebulae you will not see the colours that you get in the pictures. Check out the description of filters in Chapter 5 as these will enhance the view a little.

visually and narrowband filters will help. I have only ever seen it once, but that was through a monstrous 50 cm Dobsonian telescope under a particularly dark sky.

Not all of the fuzzy blobs you can see with your eyes will be nebulae – some of them could be distant **clusters of stars**. The constellation of Auriga has some lovely clusters within its borders and from a dark site they can look a little fuzzy to the naked eye. If you turn binoculars on them you will start to reveal some of the hundreds of stars whose combined light is reaching your eye. Stars within these clusters represent some of the youngest and oldest stars in the Universe, the youngest appearing in galactic *open clusters* like those in Auriga and the oldest in *globular clusters*. Both can be seen through binoculars but a telescope reveals their true nature.

As we have just seen, stars form through the gravitational collapse of a vast cloud of hydrogen gas. Once the stars have formed and the intense ultraviolet radiation from the hot young stars clears away the remaining nebulosity, beautiful galactic star clusters are revealed. The stars within the cluster will have their own velocity due to the random motion of the gas in the original nebula, and over millions of years the cluster will slowly disperse.

Since open clusters are the result of stellar formation, we tend to find them in the locations with the highest concentration of nebulae. This means they are usually found inside a galaxy and in particular along the plane of the spiral arms. Interestingly, it was by studying the location of open clusters that astronomers were able to deduce the shape of our Galaxy, the Milky Way, as a vast rotating spiral galaxy.

A great example of an open cluster is the Seven Sisters, or Pleiades, star cluster in the constellation Taurus. To the unaided eye it looks like seven stars (hence its name), but through a telescope up to 250 young hot stars are revealed. Images of the region even show what looks like some of the original nebulosity out of which the stars formed, but further studies have shown it is just a passing cloud of gas and dust.

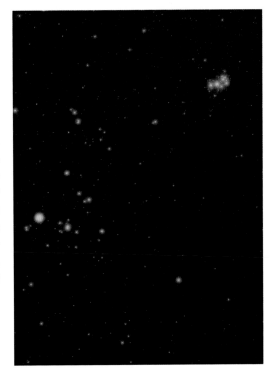

At the opposite end of the scale are the ageing globular clusters which seem to have formed at the same time as the Galaxy itself billions of years ago. Due to the lack of star-forming gas within the clusters there is barely any new star formation and so we are left with clusters of extremely old stars heading towards the end of their lives. Indeed, some of the oldest stars in the Universe have been found in globular clusters.

▶ *The Hyades and Pleiades clusters in Taurus are excellent binocular objects but can also be seen easily with the naked eye.*

Mark's observing tip for clusters

Clusters are easy to observe and there are examples that suit any instrument. One of the benefits of a telescope is that you can not only see fainter objects but you can also see finer levels of detail. This is called *resolution* and a larger telescope will have a higher resolution than a smaller one. With higher resolution you will be able to separate more individual stars in any given cluster than you could with a telescope with lower resolution. Larger telescopes can help to reveal the individual stars in globular clusters right into the core.

Unlike the open clusters, globular clusters are found in a huge halo surrounding our Galaxy. We can tell they are not unique to the Milky Way, though, as we can detect them around other galaxies too. The Andromeda Galaxy is the nearest major galaxy to our own and it has several, some of which can just be detected in large amateur telescopes. The largest known globular cluster is found just outside the Milky Way and is known as Omega Centauri, and it plays host to several million stars, compared to the typical few hundred stars in an open cluster. Unfortunately, it is only visible to observers in the southern hemisphere, but those in the northern hemisphere can enjoy views of another fine example of a globular cluster in Hercules known as M13.

▲ *The great globular cluster in Hercules, known as M13, is home to several million stars.*

All of the objects covered so far are found either in or around **galaxies** and the easiest way to visualize them is to think of a city! Cities on Earth are not physical objects but are made up from a collection of objects such as houses, cars, shops, offices, pubs, and so on. Galaxies are the same – they are not objects in their own right but are made up of stars, planets, nebulae and comets, etc, so instead can be thought of as a collection of objects that are bound together by gravity. In between the galaxies are millions of light years of empty space.

Our own Galaxy, the Milky Way, gives some idea of their scale, measuring about 100,000 light years across, with our own Solar System about two-thirds of the way out from the centre. For many years, it was thought that the Milky Way belongs to a class of galaxy called a spiral galaxy, but recent studies suggest this may not be the case. You can imagine the rough shape of a spiral galaxy by visualizing two fried eggs stuck back to back, with the yolk representing the bulge of the nucleus and the white representing the disk of the spiral arms. Galaxies come in a number of other shapes, from the spiral galaxies similar to the Andromeda Galaxy to barred spirals like our own, and from vast elliptical galaxies like the giant galaxies in the Virgo Cluster to irregular galaxies which include all the rest.

Gravity plays a big part in the life of a galaxy. It is the thing that holds it all together, but it is also the force that binds galaxies together into gigantic galactic clusters. Our own Milky Way

Galaxies

Galaxies come in a few different shapes and sizes. There are the elliptical galaxies, which tend to be home to older red stars, and the spiral or barred spiral galaxies, which have more stellar nurseries. Each type is broken into subcategories based on shape, as shown in the Hubble classification of galaxies below. The Triangulum Galaxy (*right*) is an example of a spiral galaxy.

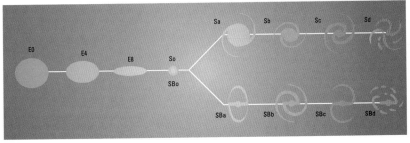

Mark's galaxy observing tip

For observing galaxies, bigger really is better. They are typically quite faint in the sky so the bigger your telescope, the brighter the image you will see and the more detail you will enjoy. Give your eyes a good hour to get dark adapted to give yourself the greatest chance of seeing them at their best.

Galaxy is a member of what we call the 'Local Group', which has about 33 members. Two of those members are our satellite galaxies, the Large and Small Magellanic Clouds which are visible from southern latitudes, and another is the Andromeda Galaxy. It is hard to appreciate the clustered nature of galaxies in our own group but the Virgo cluster of galaxies is a great example.

Some of the most distant objects visible are superbright galaxies and many of them were formed when the Universe was just a fraction of its current age. It is now thought that the powerhouse at the centre of these young galaxies is a supermassive black hole, swallowing up matter at a colossal rate. Just before the matter falls into the black hole it gets accelerated to incredible speeds, spinning round so fast that it emits a tremendous amount of energy before it gets sucked in, and it is this energy which we can detect. We now think that all galaxies, including our own Milky Way Galaxy, have black holes at their core.

▲ *The Andromeda Galaxy is the largest of our galactic neighbours and lies just over 2 million light years from us.*

▲ *There are thought to be over 2,000 members of the Virgo cluster of galaxies. Many are within easy reach of amateur telescopes and they include spiral, barred spiral and giant elliptical galaxies, just like its largest member M87.*

Everything we can see in the **Universe** – you, me, stars, planets and galaxies – are all the result of an event that happened 13.7 billion years ago. The event is known as the 'Big Bang' and it marks the moment in time when the Universe sprang into existence, seemingly from nothing! Exactly where it came from is far too great a topic for this introduction to the night sky, although I did once hear a wonderful answer by a colleague who was asked what was before the Big Bang. His answer was simple yet beautiful: 'Consider the North Pole – from here in England you can use a compass and head north. Eventually you will get there. Once you are there, you might well consider what lies further north, but in reality nothing is further north than the North Pole; you just cannot go any further and it is almost meaningless to ask what is further north than north!' His analogy was fantastic and nicely explains that while space was created in the Big Bang, we think that time was created too – so to ask what came before is meaningless because time just did not exist! It is a strange yet fascinating concept

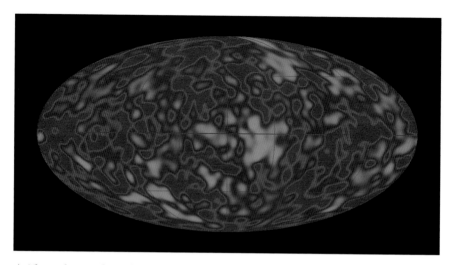

▲ *The radiation from the Big Bang can be seen in this all-sky map from COBE (Cosmic Background Explorer). It shows ripples in the microwave radiation that represent variations in temperature of just 30 millionths of a degree and it is these variations which are thought to have led to the formation of the first stars and galaxies.*

and one that is worthy of a whole book in itself, but for the purposes of this one let us just assume that by some strange mechanism the Universe popped into existence in the event known as the Big Bang.

The idea of the Big Bang is not just guesswork – it is a concept which matches real observations of the 'noise' that was discovered coming from the sky. The cosmic microwave background (CMB) radiation was discovered by two telecommunications scientists working with satellite technology. They found a strange, constant, low level of interference that seemed to be coming from all directions. Suspecting pigeon droppings in the receiver, they cleaned it out but the strange signal remained. Finally, they concluded it must be coming from the sky, and what they had unexpectedly discovered was the remnant radiation from the explosion that created our Universe. Space satellites such as COBE (Cosmic Background Explorer) can now tune in to this remnant radiation, known as the *cosmic background radiation*, and give us a glimpse at the echoes of the Big Bang.

A period of rapid expansion followed the Big Bang which allowed the Universe to cool, giving the seething mass of energy a chance to slowly change into matter. In its infancy, the Universe was composed almost entirely of hydrogen, helium and small quantities of other elements, but eventually the great clouds of hydrogen gas collapsed under the force of gravity, leading to the formation of the first generation of stars known as Population III stars. These first stars would have lived violent and short lives lasting for perhaps only a million years or so before exploding as supernovae. The explosion of these supermassive first stars would have distributed matter around the Universe, giving an opportunity for the next generation of stars known as Population II stars. As these generations of stars evolved they were working like factories to produce heavier elements deep in their core through nuclear fusion, which ultimately would lead to the formation of planets around hot young stars. There are no Population III stars visible now nor have they ever been, but it is possible to see Population II stars which generally live outside the spiral arms of our Galaxy. Many of the stars inside globular clusters are Population II while stars in the spiral arms, like the Sun, are Population I.

As the Universe evolves with stars, and perhaps life, coming and going, its fate is less than certain. Until recently we thought that the expansion of the Universe from the initial Big Bang would do one of two things depending on how much material exists (more material means more gravity). If there is a lot of material, then the total force of gravity may be enough to slow the expansion, stop it and even reverse it so the Universe starts contracting, leading to the so-called 'Big Crunch'. This event could then trigger another Big Bang and so the process may start all over again. This, of course, leads to the uncomfortable conversation again about when did it all start, but it is too much to consider in this book. It may also be that there is not quite enough gravity in the Universe to halt the expansion so it will just continue to expand forever, getting slower and slower but never quite reaching a complete halt.

Recent observations of distant supernovae have shown that the Universe is now expanding faster than it did in the past, so it seems neither the Big Crunch nor the decelerating expansion are the likely fate of the Universe. The unexpected increasing rate of expansion means there must be some previously unidentified force driving it, which is theorized to come from particles popping in and out of existence at the tiniest level. These strange and exotic particles are known as *dark energy* and their tiny pushing force is thought to be accelerating the expansion of the Universe. If that works out to be the case, and all current observations do indeed point to that fact, then the Universe will continue to expand forever, getting faster and faster until it becomes so large that all the energy and matter is so sparsely distributed that it turns into a cold dark void.

Granted, this is not a positive end to the very brief story of the evolution of the Universe, but take comfort in the fact that this will not happen for billions upon billions of years. Our Sun has been shining for just over 5 billion years and is expected to last for another 5 billion years. The really beautiful thing for me is that we can learn all this, about stars and planets and even the evolution and possible fate of the Universe, by just looking up into the night sky.

Mark's ultimate observing tip

Want to see evidence for the Big Bang yourself? If you still have access to an analogue TV then detune it from any broadcasting channel until you get the white 'snow' or hiss. This is interference that comes from various ground-based sources but not all of it! About 1% of it comes from the echoes of the Big Bang! Using an FM radio you can do the same thing by tuning out any radio stations and listening to the hiss. A small percentage of the noise that you can hear is coming from the echoes of the Big Bang, the creation of the Universe.

Abbreviation	Name	Genitive	Popular name
And	Andromeda	Andromedae	Andromeda
Ant	Antlia	Antliae	Air Pump
Aps	Apus	Apodis	Bird of Paradise
Aqr	Aquarius	Aquarii	Water Carrier
Aql	Aquila	Aquilae	Eagle
Ara	Ara	Arae	Altar
Ari	Aries	Arietis	Ram
Aur	Auriga	Aurigae	Charioteer
Boo	Boötes	Boötis	Herdsman
Cae	Caelum	Caeli	Chisel
Cam	Camelopardalis	Camelopardalis	Giraffe
Cnc	Cancer	Cancri	Crab
CVn	Canes Venatici	Canum Venaticorum	Hunting Dogs
CMa	Canis Major	Canis Majoris	Great Dog
CMi	Canis Minor	Canis Minoris	Little Dog
Cap	Capricornus	Capricorni	Sea Goat
Car	Carina	Carinae	Keel
Cas	Cassiopeia	Cassiopeiae	Cassiopeia
Cen	Centaurus	Centauri	Centaur
Cep	Cepheus	Cephei	Cepheus
Cet	Cetus	Ceti	Whale
Cha	Chamaeleon	Chamaeleontis	Chameleon
Cir	Circinus	Circini	Compasses
Col	Columba	Columbae	Dove
Com	Coma Berenices	Comae Berenicis	Berenice's Hair
CrA	Corona Australis	Coronae Australis	Southern Crown
CrB	Corona Borealis	Coronae Borealis	Northern Crown
Crv	Corvus	Corvi	Crow
Crt	Crater	Crateris	Cup
Cru	Crux	Crucis	Southern Cross
Cyg	Cygnus	Cygni	Swan
Del	Delphinus	Delphini	Dolphin
Dor	Dorado	Doradûs	Swordfish
Dra	Draco	Draconis	Dragon
Equ	Equuleus	Equulei	Foal
Eri	Eridanus	Eridani	River Eridanus
For	Fornax	Fornacis	Furnace
Gem	Gemini	Geminorum	Twins
Gru	Grus	Gruis	Crane
Her	Hercules	Herculis	Hercules

Abbreviation	Name	Genitive	Popular name
Hor	Horologium	Horologii	Clock
Hya	Hydra	Hydrae	Water Snake
Hyi	Hydrus	Hydri	Lesser Water Snake
Ind	Indus	Indi	Indian
Lac	Lacerta	Lacertae	Lizard
Leo	Leo	Leonis	Lion
LMi	Leo Minor	Leonis Minoris	Little Lion
Lep	Lepus	Leporis	Hare
Lib	Libra	Librae	Scales
Lup	Lupus	Lupi	Wolf
Lyn	Lynx	Lyncis	Lynx
Lyr	Lyra	Lyrae	Lyre
Men	Mensa	Mensae	Table Mountain
Mic	Microscopium	Microscopii	Microscope
Mon	Monoceros	Monocerotis	Unicorn
Mus	Musca	Muscae	Fly
Nor	Norma	Normae	Square
Oct	Octans	Octantis	Octant
Oph	Ophiuchus	Ophiuchi	Serpent Bearer
Ori	Orion	Orionis	Orion
Pav	Pavo	Pavonis	Peacock
Peg	Pegasus	Pegasi	Winged Horse
Per	Perseus	Persei	Perseus
Phe	Phoenix	Phoenicis	Phoenix
Pic	Pictor	Pictoris	Painter's Easel
Psc	Pisces	Piscium	Fishes
PsA	Piscis Austrinus	Piscis Austrini	Southern Fish
Pup	Puppis	Puppis	Poop
Pyx	Pyxis	Pyxidis	Ship's Compass
Ret	Reticulum	Reticuli	Net
Sge	Sagitta	Sagittae	Arrow
Sgr	Sagittarius	Sagittarii	Archer
Sco	Scorpius	Scorpii	Scorpion
Scl	Sculptor	Sculptoris	Sculptor
Sct	Scutum	Scuti	Shield
Ser	Serpens	Serpentis	Serpent
Sex	Sextans	Sextantis	Sextant
Tau	Taurus	Tauri	Bull
Tel	Telescopium	Telescopii	Telescope
Tri	Triangulum	Trianguli	Triangle
TrA	Triangulum Australe	Trianguli Australis	Southern Triangle
Tuc	Tucana	Tucanae	Toucan
UMa	Ursa Major	Ursae Majoris	Great Bear
UMi	Ursa Minor	Ursae Minoris	Little Bear
Vel	Vela	Velorum	Sails
Vir	Virgo	Virginis	Virgin
Vol	Volans	Volantis	Flying Fish
Vul	Vulpecula	Vulpeculae	Fox

INDEX